"One of the most urgent questions facing today's generation of young Christians is this—does God really intend for us to make marriage a priority? Confusion reigns in this area of the Christian life. Far too many young Christians sideline marriage, delay marriage, and avoid marriage in an extension of adolescence that is truly unique in human history. Now comes Debbie Maken with sound advice, serious thinking, and an honest approach to this question that will help all Christians think about our responsibility to get serious about getting married. This book should be a must-read for all Christian young adults—and for all who love them."

—R. ALBERT MOHLER, JR., president,
The Southern Baptist Theological Seminary

"This book will be life-changing for the singles who read this, as Debbie so aptly pokes holes in all those evangelical church myths about why singles should be 'content.'"

—JULIA DUIN, assistant national editor,
The Washington Times

DEBBIE MAKEN

RETHINKING THE GIFT OF SINGLENESS

Getting Serious ABOUT Getting Married

CROSSWAY BOOKS

A PUBLISHING MINISTRY OF
GOOD NEWS PUBLISHERS
WHEATON, ILLINOIS

Library of Congress Cataloging-in-Publication Data
Maken, Debbie, 1970–
   Getting serious about getting married / Debbie Maken.
     p. cm.
   ISBN 13: 978-1-58134-741-8
   ISBN 10: 1-58134-741-3 (tpb)
   1. Marriage—Religious aspects—Christianity. 2. Marriage—Biblical teaching. I. Title
BV835.M2245   2005
248.4—dc22   2005022083

ML		16	15	14	13	12	11	10	09	08	07	06
15	14	13	12	11	10	9	8	7	6	5	4	3	2	1

For my daughters, Hannah and Abigail
May you grow up
into a time
when godly suitors abound

Contents

Acknowledgments

No author ever comes to this point without the support, love, understanding, and encouragement of many people. First, I want to thank my husband for his love and for being my covering. Thank you for our wonderful life together and the beautiful children you have helped me bring into this world. They make this book even more necessary.

I also want to thank my own mother, Chhanda, and my mother-in-law, Pam, for the countless hours of baby-sitting and praying for this message. And thanks to both of my children for their sacrifice of "mommy time" as I labored to finish this project.

Thank you to the many friends who have read several different versions of this book for their honesty, candor, and encouragement. I especially thank Rebecca Anthony whose daily struggle with extended singleness reminds me that the fight is not over. I also want to thank other "eyes" that helped along the way: Bob Frey, Kari Foster, Elizabeth Maron, and countless others. Thanks also to all those who sent me research materials and to those friends who prayed for the success of this message, including (but not limited to) Susan Moates and Stephanie Lee. May God reward you for your goodness to me.

I want to thank Crossway Books for seeing the need for this message and Bill Jensen for seeing me as an Esther with a message "for such a time as this." I want to thank my editor, Joanne Heim, for her efforts in directing my pen to appeal to this generation of single women I care so greatly about. Thanks to my agent, Matt Jacobson, and his team for all of their efforts in giving a first-time author "a break" and circulating this manuscript.

I am ever so grateful to all of you.

Introduction:
Confessions of an "Almost" Spinster

Their young women had no marriage song.

PSALM 78:63

When I was in my early twenties, I didn't really mind being single; after all, my life was full. I had a successful career as an up-and-coming attorney. I liked my family, church, and friends. I had a nice car and an active social life. I was involved in various civic and church ministries. I had a beautiful home and was decorating it to my heart's content. As the saying goes, I was cute enough, smart enough, and—don't you know it—people liked me. The one thing I didn't have was a husband, but I considered that only a minor inconvenience that time would fix.

Like most other young women I knew, I had a series of rotating boyfriends—mostly frogs who refused to become princes—and I figured I'd eventually meet the "right one." In the meantime I gave myself spiritual pep talks and claimed God's promises. I reasoned that God, the Sovereign of the universe, could change my single state if he wanted to and that it certainly hadn't escaped his notice.

I stuffed deep down any nagging thought of being permanently husbandless, sexless, and childless. This kind of trained ignorance ("Don't think about it, Debbie!") worked for a while. But eventually the cycle of good days and bad days turned into good weeks and bad weeks, followed by years, until almost a decade had passed. This false hope couldn't be sustained indefinitely. Just as a party balloon shrinks and falls over time, my confidence and hope had deflated by my late twenties.

What has changed? I wondered. My lifestyle was pretty much the same—same house, car, furnishings, family, and friends. But that was the

11

problem—it was all the same. My life had not expanded to include a husband or children. The weight of what I lacked began to feel oppressive.

Why wasn't I content anymore? This was a question I hardly dared to ask because I knew being discontent about my single status just wasn't allowed. Raising poignant questions about singleness came with the guarantee of an onslaught of trite platitudes and glib, pithy sayings. "It's better to be single than to wish you were." "Marriage is a lot harder than it looks." "Bloom where you're planted." "It might not be God's will for you to marry." "God knows when you will be ready, and he'll send you a husband at just the right time." "Think of all the ways you can serve God by being single." Knowing what I would hear, I pretended I was happy with my singleness, though in actuality I was totally miserable inside.

I still went to church and was growing in my relationship with God. I even took leadership roles in the singles activities at church. I continued to attend the singles Sunday school class, just as I'd been doing since I was twenty-one. But I remembered something I'd noticed then. As I looked around at women sporting telltale signs of age, I remembered wondering, *Shouldn't these women have graduated from this class by now? Shouldn't they be in the married group or the young family group?* But not knowing a thing about them, I had shrugged off that ominous feeling and just assumed there had to be a good reason why they were still single.

Then one Sunday morning I arrived at Sunday school, smiling on the outside, yet depressed inside. At twenty-eight, I was now one of those women I'd wondered about at twenty-one. That year had marked the end of yet another disappointing dating relationship. I'd also spent the previous few months helping a family struggle through placing their first grandchild up for adoption when their college-aged daughter had become pregnant. For the past year I'd been hearing a quiet voice whisper, *There has to be a better way to arrive at the altar than through all this hurt.*

That morning as I sat down, I thought to myself, *There's absolutely no reason for me to be here in this singles class. I don't even like being single! I'm not content with this.* As soon as I uttered this thought in my heart, I caught myself. *No, that's not what I'm feeling. This can't be possible.* And then I thought it again. *I am NOT content. No, no, NO!,* I yelled in my head. *I'm unhappy and sad about still being single.*

I couldn't believe I was thinking these things. I tried to take such wayward thoughts captive as Paul taught in the New Testament, but the next thing I knew I was telling myself, *I'm not only discontent—I am also angry about being single.* I told myself, *It's time to leave.* So I got up, left that room, and thought, *I'm never going back.*

I poured out my heart to God that morning. I finally admitted to my Maker that I was dating-wearied, lonely, depressed, frustrated, and, yes, terrified of the future. I started to ask him some serious questions. If the last ten years hadn't brought any serious marriage prospects, what guarantee did I have that the next ten years would prove any better, especially since I wasn't getting any younger? At this rate, would I still be able to have children if I married too late? If I grew old alone, who would take care of me? Would a weekly girls' night out and a few occasional dates be it for the rest of my life? These are the confessions of someone who almost became a Christian spinster. Sadly, I'm not the only one who's felt like this. We live in a day when this is the story of many modern women, Christian or not.

At twenty-eight I found myself sandwiched between younger single girlfriends and older ones. My friend Jackie was twenty-two and not yet very concerned with the fact that she was single. After all, she was still fairly young and had just started graduate school. She was cute and went out on dates from time to time. While she enjoyed dating to some extent, she admitted that it was not nearly as much fun as it looked on television. She had definite plans to get married and have children someday, but *someday* was still a ways off. But even Jackie was beginning to wonder when Mr. Right would appear. If he was out there, she hadn't met him yet, nor any of his distant cousins. The guys she'd dated as an adult so far just didn't seem to be husband material. To be honest, they were more concerned with acquiring toys than a family.

At the other end, my friend Rachel had just turned thirty-six. She was now very, very depressed and concerned about her continued singleness. When she was thirty-three, she had even decided to move to a bigger city in a different state, hoping that a higher population of single people would improve her chances of meeting Mr. Right. So far this hope hadn't materialized. She'd been left with a total of three dates in three years, and one eHarmony match that had fizzled out without explanation. Waiting for men to ask her out was no fun, and she was starting to feel desperate and rather like an old maid. All her single life she'd heard that Jesus was all she needed to be happy; she had her doubts. Other friends—married friends—told her that marriage wasn't all it's cracked up to be, and sex really wasn't all that great either. Confused and lonely, she felt like life was passing her by. Her relationship with God was strong and growing, but she wasn't convinced that God really wanted her to remain single. If he did, why was she hurting so much?

I realized that I couldn't go back to age twenty-two like Jackie and get those six years back to redo things in hopes that I'd be married by twenty-eight. I also realized that in eight more years I could be in my mid-thirties like Rachel, still single and unhappy, with no change in my marital status.

When I walked out of that Sunday school class and vowed never to return, it was my way of saying, "Enough is enough!" I knew that the "same old, same old" of being single wouldn't satisfy me any longer. There was no going back into pretended contentment. Why should I continue doing things just as before—going to singles Sunday school class, doing all the "right" things, and sitting like a bump on a log waiting for some random man to come along and change my destiny? It was time for a change. A big change. Not a new hairstyle or color. Not a new pair of shoes. Not a new self-help book for single women. I had to understand why my generation was chronically single, and if this was something I could overcome or whether I would remain an unwitting hostage to a less than desirable fate. That journey became this book.

My story has a happy ending. I met my husband in July 2001, became engaged later that same year, and married in March 2002. We live a comfortable life in sunny Florida, have two daughters, and hope to have more children in the years ahead. How I arrived at the altar is a fascinating story, one I'll share later in the book. But at the risk of this coming off as just another how-to book, I think the better story lies within how my thinking changed in such a radical way that I was able to get married while time was still on my side. Of course, changing your thinking is not a guarantee that a husband will appear quickly or even appear at all. But it will increase your chances of being married because you will be part of a movement emerging in the Christian world. I see it on the horizon as we are beginning to recapture the truth of Scripture on marriage, and that gives me hope.

Perhaps you're wondering why I continued with this book once I got married. Upon hearing of my engagement, one woman at church said to me, "I guess you can put down your pen now." As if my engagement had solved the problem facing single women today! The issue goes beyond just my experience.

According to the United States Census Bureau, just one generation ago, in the 1970s, approximately 64 percent of women had married by age twenty-four, roughly 90 percent had married by age twenty-nine, and 94 percent by age thirty-four. Just thirty years later, approximately 27 percent of women have married by age twenty-four, approximately 60 percent by age twenty-nine, and 78 percent by age thirty-four.[1] The singles population has *tripled* or *quadrupled* in just one generation! I knew there had to be an explanation for this other than God just wanting more "gifted singles" in this generation. The reason I am so passionate about the message of this book is because it is not just about me; it is about the countless untold stories of women who are dying on the vine, know it, and feel like they can't do a thing about it.

In a way, the day I exited the singles Sunday school class was the beginning of the rest of my life. What I learned that morning was that the feelings I had bottled up weren't going to stay bottled up any longer. I had to acknowledge them, confront them, and deal with them. I had to examine their source and determine if these feelings were coming from me, Satan, or God.

I asked the Lord to search my heart and reveal why I was balking against my singleness, against a state I had thought he wanted for me. What God showed me was that I had used most of my twenties to master avoidance, not true spiritual peace. Even more interesting was that he showed me that I was never going to get true spiritual peace about singleness because I wasn't called to singleness, and the Spirit does not give peace about something that is outside of God's calling. God taught me that it was never his intention for people to be single for such protracted amounts of time and that if I continued on this same path, I could only expect further disappointment and hurt in the years ahead.

I am writing this book because I believe what God taught me during the four years following my walk-out will help not only this generation of Christian single women but also the generation to come, which includes my own daughters, Hannah and Abigail.

I spent countless hours during those years studying Scripture, reading contemporary books on dating and courtship, and researching what the church has historically believed regarding marriage and singleness. The things I learned may be surprising and even shocking for today's Christian world—for what I learned challenges virtually everything a Christian single woman living today has been taught regarding marriage and singleness. I also imagine that what I learned and want to share with you will garner some resistance because it goes against the grain of modern thinking.

Let me assure you that what I've learned and what I'm writing about—no matter how radical it may sound at first—is based squarely upon the Bible and was accepted by Christian thinkers for centuries as the prevailing wisdom. As you read, let Scripture be your measuring stick for truth—not psychology, not culture, not what you've accepted thus far, not what sounds good or catchy. There is benefit in understanding where we as a church and as a culture have gone wrong. As the saying goes, those who don't learn from history are doomed to repeat it. Knowing the truth offers the hope of freedom.

We have been told over and over that singleness is a gift. But it's the kind of gift that makes us cringe and smile politely while we desperately search for a gift receipt so we can return it. It's like receiving a sequined sweater that doesn't match anything in our closet, or a Christmas fruitcake. Despite this common attitude, we are conditioned to accept singleness as a gift from God and to be content. Our singleness, we're told, is not up for negotiation.

I want to share with you that this teaching on singleness is a new one—and a radical departure from classical Christian thought that for centuries viewed marriage as the rule for everyone, with only a few exceptions. Christian tradition has never validated wholesale singleness. To the contrary, virtually all of our Christian forefathers regarded protracted singleness as unbiblical and believed that young adults were under a divine duty to marry without undue delay. And this old idea had consequences—there was very little singleness. Because of this belief, parents and society maintained systems that facilitated marriage, and men aspired to achieve biblical masculinity by actively searching and pursuing wives in a timely manner—sooner rather than later.

Our new teaching on singleness also has consequences—it is, in part, responsible for costing young women marriage. Any young man who is currently taught that singleness is a gift equal to marriage will have very little incentive to press forward and make a real home by taking on the real responsibilities of a wife and children.

In today's contemporary church, we not only suffer from historical amnesia, we use faulty and erroneous theology to make something abnormal look like it is a sanctified gift straight from the hand of God. We are so conditioned to validate and affirm everyone that we don't have the kindness to tell them when something—in this case, singleness—is actually detrimental to their whole lives. In so doing, we have developed a giant blind spot to the high costs of remaining single indefinitely.

According to Dr. Sanjay Gupta, a neurosurgeon and CNN medical correspondent, singles, from a health standpoint, have a higher rate of alcoholism, suicide, depression, and heart disease.[2] Linda Waite and Maggie Gallagher in *The Case for Marriage* have found that singles also have a lower level of income than their married counterparts.[3]

The National Marriage Project, an organization providing research and analysis on the state of marriage in America, has found that "in general, marital delay leaves young adults with an increased exposure to the hazards of nonmarital sex and childbearing, sexual exploitation, loneliness, and a lack of social integration."[4] Being a single person for too long has more capacity to produce negative characteristics in terms of sanctification than it does to produce healthy members of the body of Christ. And yet we persist in our churches to praise the single status, placing it on an equal level with marriage. We delude ourselves and the singles in our congregations into believing that participation in a few service activities will somehow redeem or offset all of the negative practical—and sometimes spiritual—consequences of remaining single despite God's clear call to marriage.

Condoning singleness from the pulpit is in large part responsible for causing singles to resign themselves to their unfortunate and less-than-ideal fate. With the benefits of marriage systematically downplayed and the supposed freedoms and hyper-sanctification of the single lifestyle glorified, protracted singleness becomes a self-fulfilling prophecy. I believe that the greatest challenge in regard to singleness for the church today is honesty—not flattery of something that goes against the truth of God's Word.

I am writing this book because we, as the people of God, have been walking around in circles on this issue for the last twenty years or so. The church has failed to offer meaningful alternatives to ongoing singleness or even a good understanding of why protracted singleness runs rampant in our society. My goal is not to condemn the church but to encourage and challenge the church—and us as her members—to change her thinking and teaching about singleness and marriage.

Together we will examine God's purpose for marriage and see the cultural shift that has moved thinking about marriage and singleness away from what God intended. Then we'll identify messages about singleness from both church and culture and replace faulty thinking with truth straight from the Word of God. Finally, we'll learn how to live honestly and increase our chances of marriage by changing how we pursue the goal of marriage, a calling that God intends for us as his people.

Discussion questions are included at the end of the book to spark conversation and further explore the ideas you'll discover as you read this book. I'm excited to share my journey with you and to show you what God has taught me about what went wrong in the quest for marriage. So grab a girlfriend or two, and let's get serious about getting married!

PART 1

Marriage

AND

Singleness

CHAPTER 1

What the Bible Says About Marriage

The path to the altar hasn't always been as filled with pitfalls and dangers as it is today. The problems that beset us crept in slowly with a shift toward modern thinking. Surprisingly, much of this change happened in our lifetime. My hope in writing this book is that we can get rid of those problems in the same way—with a revolution in thinking.

The truth is, previous generations saw marriage and singleness very differently than we do today, and that affected how they approached life. We don't need a time machine to zap us back to 1822; what we do need is to discover what these Christian cultures believed and then renew our own thinking to get back to where they were. And their thinking about these issues was based squarely upon the Bible.

So let's go back to the beginning and see what God intended when he created marriage. As the one who came up with the idea, God knows more about marriage than any other source. He is more reliable, more accurate, and more truthful about marriage and its purpose than anyone or anything else we may find.

The very first recorded account of marriage is found in Genesis 1—3. These chapters spell out exactly what God intended when he created marriage. We discover that he instituted marriage in the Garden of Eden—before sin entered the picture—for a number of reasons. But before we look at those reasons, let's talk about marriage and God's will.

MARRIAGE IS GOD'S WILL

Often I hear singles fret, "But I don't know if it's God's will for me to get married! After all, if it was God's will, wouldn't I be married by now?" As I've talked with close friends about God's will and marriage, what it's boiled down to is that because they're not married now (and often don't see any prospects in the near future) they conclude that God must not want them to get married. If you're assuming that God wants you to be single because you are, let me offer some encouragement. God's will is not dependent on your circumstances or our culture or the guy you dated last year, last month, or last Friday night. God's will is dependent upon God alone and is revealed in Scripture by what he's declared to be his divine intention.

Unfortunately, God's will is often presented as a big unknown—something that only theologians (or at least seminary students) can discern with accuracy. But God's will at its most basic level is simply what God intends or desires. One of the primary ways we discern God's will for our lives is by reading the Bible—something anyone can do. In his Word, God reveals his character and his purposes for his people.

The Bible tells us that Jesus is "the same yesterday and today and forever" (Hebrews 13:8). James 1:17 says that God does not change. What we learn about him from the Bible—whether in Genesis, Joel, or James—is just as relevant for us today as it was in the past.

The Bible is clear: _It is God's will for people to marry_. (There are, of course, exceptions to the rule, but we'll get to that in the next chapter.) That's my purpose for writing this book—to help us as the people of God move back to a biblical view of marriage as God created it. Genesis 1:26-28 and 2:8-25 reveal that God mandated marriage not just for his people, but for the entire world. Marriage remains God's _revealed_ will (revealed in his Word, the Bible, as what he wants), even if as a culture we have made its attainment an elusive, secret, perpetual guessing game. Scripture states that "God created man in his own image . . . male and female he created them" (Genesis 1:27). This means that the male-female union is for God's own glory; marriage reflects his image far better than either sex individually. Because God made us "male and female," we were neither designed nor intended to be completed only by God on this side of heaven; the full expression of maleness and femaleness is found in marriage, not merely in relationships with other individuals.

Marriage reflects God's glory. Dr. Albert Mohler of the Southern Baptist Theological Seminary says it should "never be seen as mere human invention—an option for those who choose such a high level of commitment—for it is an arena in which God's glory is displayed."[1] The male-female partnership is to be viewed as serving the purposes of God.[2] So what else does the Bible say about why marriage exists?

Marriage Keeps Us from Being Alone

Being single is lonely. Despite a successful career, great friends, and a growing relationship with the Lord, I was lonely. Though my friends and I were told we were "whole" and "complete" on our own, we knew something was missing and we longed for it—we *yearned* for it.

The reason for this yearning is found in Genesis. The Bible doesn't say that God made us male *or* female, but that he made us in his image, male *and* female. Theologian and reformer John Calvin commented:

> When he soon afterwards adds, that God created them "male and female," he commends us to that conjugal bond by which the society of mankind is cherished. For this form of speaking, "God created man, male and female he created them," is of the same force as if he had said that man himself was incomplete.[3]

God was saying that man—on his own, without woman—was incomplete. God said, "It is not good that the man should be alone" (2:18). He declared this "not good" on the heels of six pronouncements of "good" and one "very good" in the creation account.

This doesn't come as much of a surprise. The majority of single women I meet enjoy their singleness about as much as I did—which is to say, not very much at all. To flip a phrase on its head, I enjoyed my singleness about as much as a fish would enjoy a bicycle! That thought is actually a reflection of the heart of our Maker—it simply is "not good for [woman] to be alone." Calvin said that a man without a woman is but "half a man."[4] The reason we feel a lack of wholeness is because *God designed us to feel incomplete without a spouse.* God himself called the state of singleness "not good." By being dissatisfied with singleness, we're simply agreeing with God!

Many critics jump in at this point and argue that marriage isn't always a cure for loneliness. They point out that many people feel lonely in marriage. True. Marriage does not make all of our troubles disappear. However, we must remember that "the blessing of God" (in this case, marriage) often does not "flourish" because, as Calvin said, the "order of nature . . . has been inverted by us" in the entrance of sin.[5] In other words, because of sin, nothing is as it should be.

But it is always better for us to order our lives according to God's principles than to be held back because others have failed. In this case, it is better to live by what God has intended in regard to marriage than to miss out on its intended fullness because we've seen some unhappy marriages. Just because someone else failed doesn't mean we will. Think of all we'd miss if we refused to try based on others' failure! Reformation theologian Martin Luther agreed with Calvin that when God said,

> It is not good . . . [this means that] God knows what is better for you than you yourself. . . . If you deem it otherwise . . . you neither understand nor believe God's word and work. See, with this statement of God one stops the mouths of all those who criticize and censure marriage.[6]

God knows best; we must believe him.

When we look at Genesis, the reason that we are in a world of hurt is obvious. We've been stuck in a state that was neither God's desire nor intention for us! As offspring of Adam and Eve, we too were made with a spouse-shaped hole that only a husband can occupy. Had God intended a buddy system of friends and family to be a happy compromise in the fight against aloneness, he could have simply made more people from the available dust and removed Adam's loneliness through community. Adam's new friends could have helped him care for the garden and exercise dominion over the animals. Adam's mind could have been distracted from his aloneness with more activities, perhaps more animals to name.

But God didn't choose any of these options. Therefore, it's safe to conclude that God's plan was to remove Adam's loneliness (and ours as his offspring) through a spouse, not through friends or community. Don't get me wrong—friends and community are wonderful and have their place. My life wouldn't be nearly as rich without their presence. But marriage was created specifically to relieve our loneliness; marriage is God's intended choice for fixing the problem of being alone. We can substitute friends in a small group, submerse ourselves in our professions, pile program upon program onto our lives, but at the end of the day the loneliness doesn't go away. Believe me, I tried, but it didn't work for long.

Of course, dealing with loneliness wasn't God's only reason for creating marriage. He wanted Adam to have "a helper" in his work, and he wanted them to "be fruitful and multiply" (see Genesis 1:28; 2:18). Let's look at each of those purposes in turn.

MARRIAGE GIVES MEANING TO WORK

After God made Adam, he sent him straight to work. The work God ordained for him didn't just get important things done like naming all the animals—it revealed his need for a partner. When Moses (the author of Genesis) sighed, "there was not found a helper fit [suitable] for him" (2:20), you almost want to ask, "Did he expect to find a suitable helper among the animals?" Well, of course not! But the negative answer that seems so obvious to us may not have been as obvious to Adam; it wasn't until God told Adam to name the animals that Adam realized he was alone. In other words, God ordered Adam's work to make him see his aloneness. God first ordained work for the man specifically but ordained marriage for both man and woman, with the understanding that the man would find the helper he needed to do his work through marriage.[7] According to Genesis, then, work is secondary to marriage—work has a goal beyond the work itself.[8]

Here's what I mean. As a single woman I often had a hard time making it to work some mornings. And it wasn't just a lack of caffeine. I knew I was called to be a lawyer because of my gifts and talents, but boy, did the enthusiasm for work wane after a while! I found myself asking the same questions over and over: What's it all for? *Who* is it all for? These questions kept popping up because God designed work to benefit family. Without someone to work for, work is just a hollow exercise. God did not design work for us to satisfy our bosses or only to support ourselves.

The money we earn from work shouldn't be spent on self-centered consumerism or by people we don't even know. God designed work as a way for us to make an inheritance for our children.

In today's world, work and marriage often end up on two sides of an argument. But work and marriage were not meant to be competitors. Marriage was intended to allow people to work better and to prosper together.

Adam understood the delicate balance between doing God's work and having a helper in his spouse. When presented with Eve, he was totally lost in awe of her. "This at last is bone of bones and flesh of my flesh," he said (Genesis 2:23). In other words, "Wow!" He didn't say, "I was wondering when the help would get here." He didn't protest that he didn't have time for a wife after all his tiring duties of gardening and naming the animals. In his unbroken fellowship with God, Adam recognized that God had provided him a wife to be his helper, not to add another burden to his litany of duties.

While some men today do want and pursue marriage, there are also those who flinch at the prospect of marriage, viewing a wife and family as drains on their bank accounts rather than as gifts God designed for their benefit. They protest finding a wife with the excuse that they're too busy working. Worse, many often hold a series of menial jobs, living at home with parents, pretending they can't support a wife, and yet they have enough disposable income for expensive electronics, travel, and other hobbies.[9]

At the same time, the social science data from Linda Waite and Maggie Gallagher in *The Case for Marriage* prove the Genesis point because married men enjoy more monetary success than single men and climb the corporate ladder more quickly, enjoying better health and living longer.[10] How's that for a response to the next guy you date who pales at the mention of marriage?

MARRIAGE WAS DESIGNED FOR THE CREATION OF LEGITIMATE CHILDREN

God also created marriage to produce children. As one pastor/writer has said, "Marriage is a covenantal union, designed by God with a set purpose in mind—and that purpose is a fruitful covenantal union."[11] This is what God meant when he told Adam and Eve to "be fruitful and multiply" (1:28). In other words, make babies!

Of course, babies are born without the benefit of marriage every day. But God designed sex—and the babies who result from sex—for marriage alone. I'm not going to get into the how's and why's of that here; that's not what this book is about. Since we're looking at marriage as God created it, we're going to set aside the ways in which we as sinful people have twisted God's plan to suit our own needs throughout time and history and instead look at what the Bible says about why marriage was created.

Malachi 2:15 reminds us of this purpose for marriage: "Did he not make them one, with a portion of the Spirit in their union? And what was the one God seeking? Godly offspring. So guard yourselves in your spirit, and let none of you be faithless to the wife of your youth." God created us as sexual beings not only to enjoy sex, but also to create more people who bear his own image. (Genesis 5:1, 3 tells us, "When God created man, he made him in the likeness of God. . . . Adam . . . fathered a son in his own likeness, after his image.") As we bear children, we pass on God's image to them. Even putting Christian revelation aside, a purely secular understanding of natural law confirms the superiority and the rationale for the male-female ordering. Natural law simply means that "the way something is made is the way it should act."[12] All of nature testifies that people and animals come together and group according to their kind in order to be fruitful and multiply.

Because we are the children of Adam and Eve, we retain their genetic coding of being built for intimacy with someone of the opposite sex on both a physical and emotional level. We retain their need to marry for the same reasons. The Puritans preached that marriage was created for the purpose of "mutual society, help, and comfort," and secondarily for the procreation of children.[13]

LET'S LIVE AS GOD INTENDED

When we ignore the fact that God made marriage for our benefit in these ways, we deny our very nature. God created us for marriage. The reason singleness is disappointing, lets us down, and leaves us wanting more is because singleness isn't what God intended.

Stick with me here. Singleness is unnatural—it goes against our very nature. (Think back to the definition of natural law we just read.) No wonder so many single women feel lost and alone! No wonder as singleness goes on (and on and on), we don't become better at handling it.

I don't know about you, but for me, being single just got worse and worse. I didn't become the "dynamic" single that Christian books on singleness promised me I could be. Instead of reaching some sort of singleness nirvana, I realized I was being tricked into denying my very self by pretending to be happy with my single life. Calvin remarked that when men and women are not "connected [in marriage], they are like the mutilated members of a mangled body."[14]

God made the woman for the man (1 Corinthians 11:8). Similarly, God designed the human body to live with oxygen. If oxygen is slowly depleted, the human body might adjust to the strain at first. But if the oxygen content continues to lower as time progresses, the body eventually dies because it is fighting—unsuccessfully—against its design to need oxygen.

I'm not trying to make you feel bad—I promise! I want to be honest and identify that the reason so many of us have balked at the suffocation of singleness is because we have wanted to breathe normally and deeply as God intended. *We don't want to be alone because God doesn't want us to be alone.* We want the fruit of our labors to benefit our own families as God intended. We want sexual intimacy with husbands as God intended. We want legitimate children as God intended.

When you feel suffocated by your singleness, don't deny it or rearrange your life with substitutes. It didn't work for me, and it won't work for you. Acknowledge what God intended, and move forward with honesty.

CHAPTER 2

What the Bible Says About Being Single

After the last chapter, I know what's coming. "But people *are* single, despite what God wants. After all, even people in the Bible were single. What about the apostle Paul? He was single. And God certainly seemed to approve of him!" Good questions.

When we approach Scripture, we must look at it as a whole. It's a story with a beginning, middle, and end; no one section makes perfect sense without the others. Scripture always validates Scripture, and we must balance what God established in Genesis with what the rest of the Bible says in order to arrive at one coherent, noncontradictory, whole understanding.

So does the Bible validate singleness? If so, where and under what circumstances? After lots of study, I've found that *Scripture does not categorically authorize singleness.* It does allow singleness for a limited few and establishes clear parameters by which they can be legitimately single (see Matthew 19:4-11 and 1 Corinthians 7). The converse then is also true: People who don't meet the singleness requirements are under the general rule of marriage that God established in Genesis.

There are many single people in the world—and in the church— today. By some measures over a quarter of the population in America today is considered single. But can all of these millions of single people legitimately remain single long-term according to Scripture? Let's start with what Jesus had to say on the subject.

JESUS WAS PRO-MARRIAGE

In Matthew 19:4-11 Jesus addressed the issue of marriage when the Pharisees tried to trap him in a debate between two schools of thought on divorce. One group permitted divorce for a wide range of reasons (going back to the time of Moses); the other had stricter rules concerning when divorce was permissible. In response, Jesus pointed them back to Genesis:

> *He answered, "Have you not read that he who created them from the beginning made them male and female, and said, 'Therefore a man shall leave his father and his mother and hold fast to his wife, and they shall become one flesh'? So they are no longer two but one flesh. What therefore God has joined together, let not man separate." (Matthew 19:4-6)*

By going back to the beginning, Jesus was saying that God had not changed his mind about marriage. Then he answered their specific question, telling them that adultery is a biblical reason for divorce (Matthew 19:9; 1 Corinthians 7:13-15 adds desertion by an unbelieving spouse as the only other biblical reason for divorce). Matthew 19 confirms God's purpose for making us "male and female"—to reflect his image most completely through unity in marriage. By basically limiting justification for divorce to adultery, commentator Craig Blomberg states, Jesus "restores the law of marriage to its original basis."[1] He goes on to say that the "creation ordinance [of marriage] remains in effect even after the fall of the human race, the giving of the law, and the coming of the kingdom with Jesus."[2]

Jesus was clearly pro-marriage.

I've heard the argument that comes next, and I'm sure you have too. "But Jesus was single!" Let's not justify being single just because Jesus was! There are a lot of things that Jesus was and did that we are *never* going to be or do. He was born to a virgin mother, he was the Son of God, he never sinned, he walked on water, he healed the sick and raised the dead, he died to save us, he rose from the dead, and he ascended into heaven where he is now seated at the right hand of God interceding on our behalf. There's no reason for us to "single out" (bad pun, I know!)

his single status to copy since we're not going to take on the rest of his duties too. Philosopher-theologian Desiderius Erasmus wrote, "As if indeed there [are] not very many aspects of Christ's life which should excite our wonder rather than our imitation."[3]

So what else do we learn from this passage?

WELL, MAYBE WE'LL JUST STAY SINGLE THEN

After listening to this exchange between Jesus and the Pharisees, the disciples realized the weight of Jesus' teaching about marriage. Marriage is permanent, Jesus said, except in the case of adultery. With this realization, they decided that they were willing to forego marriage and stay single. "If such is the case of a man with his wife, it is better not to marry" (Matthew 19:10).

Sounds familiar, doesn't it? I can't count all the times I was told by my married friends that marriage really isn't all that great and that I should be glad to be single rather than trapped by marriage. That's exactly what the disciples were saying here.

But Jesus had an answer for that argument too. Remember, the problem with the Pharisees' concept of marriage was that it was a contract that could be unilaterally modified by the reneging spouse; they wanted all of the benefits of marriage but none of the burdens. The disciples' reasoning reflected the flip side of the coin; they didn't want the burdens, so they were willing to forego the benefits. The disciples argued in favor of permanent singleness as an escape route to the problems inevitable in a marriage relationship. Jesus wasted no time in correcting the withdrawal-from-marriage mentality:

"Not everyone can receive this saying, but only those to whom it is given. For there are eunuchs who have been so from birth, and there are eunuchs who have been made eunuchs by men, and there are eunuchs who have made themselves eunuchs for the sake of the kingdom of heaven. Let the one who is able to receive this receive it." (Matthew 19:11-12)

Essentially Jesus was saying, "Hang on a second!" Most people have not been given the word to remain single—we're not designed by God to forgo sex. Jesus affirmed that God made us sexual beings with physical needs to drive us to marriage.

In his response to the disciples, Jesus argued against singleness as a philosophy or way of life. The only exception Jesus acknowledged is for those who have received a clear direction from God to be single ("for the sake of the kingdom of heaven") or those whose physical design, whether by birth or injury, precludes their participation in marriage. Martin Luther stated that only these three groups were exempted from the creation ordinance of marriage, and "apart from these three groups, let no man presume to be without a spouse."[4]

SO, WHAT KIND OF EUNUCH ARE YOU?

I once went on a date with a thirty-seven-year-old bachelor. Curious about why he was still single at that age, I asked him, "So, what kind of 'eunuch' are you?" I know it's not your typical conversation starter on a first date, but I wasn't going to waste my time dating someone who wasn't looking for marriage.

Needless to say, he wasn't thrilled with the question. In fact, he was angry that I dared to question his status as a single person. We talked about singleness according to the Bible—that if he was legitimately single, he'd either been called to be single for full-time kingdom work that made family life impossible, as it was with Paul and Jeremiah, or he must have a medical file somewhere that proved he was exempt from marriage because he was unable to perform its duties. If either of those two things were true, he had no business dating me or anyone else.

He believed I had a right to ask him about his virginity (something that seems much more personal to me), but that it was "none of my business" which kind of eunuch he was.

I told him that the differences separating the two issues were slim—both questions were ones of accountability. He preferred to give an account of his sexual activity, but not for having a protracted singleness.

What this guy and many other men in our generation fail to see is that being single without meeting the necessary criteria set out in Matthew 19 is just as unbiblical as sexual activity outside of marriage. John Calvin went so far to say that any man who, without the gift of "continence" (celibacy), failed to secure a wife was guilty of "stealing" a husband from a wife![5]

To this generation that believes we have the right to grow at our own pace, to remain in school indefinitely, to live a financially unconstrained and immature life, to play the field without pursuing marriage, this idea is totally foreign. We're conditioned to believe that these are personal decisions affecting only ourselves, and we fail to see the impact that this kind of "me first" lifestyle has on others. The Bible, however, does not excuse this kind of singleness and calls us to something more.

So what kind of singleness *is* excused?

The first type of eunuch Jesus described represents those who were born deformed, those who are too weak or not equipped by nature to have sex or to father children. They are exempt from marriage because God made them that way.

The second kind of eunuch is one who was castrated by men. As Luther said, they are "set apart from the natural ordinance to be fruitful and multiply, though only by an act of violence."[6] It was customary in certain cultures to castrate men who acted as guards to protect a king's harem; these men would be excused from marriage.

The third group of eunuchs is what Luther said "categorically consist[s] of those spiritually rich and exalted persons, bridled by the grace of God . . . who [would rather] beget spiritual children. Such persons are *rare, not one in a thousand*, for they are a special miracle of God. No one should venture on such a life unless he be specifically called by God, like Jeremiah."[7]

These are individuals who have been called to do some kind of kingdom work that simply won't accommodate a family. They would include people like Mother Teresa in India, or pioneer missionary David Brainerd who traveled up and down Delaware ministering to the Indians until he died. These are people who use their *entire* lives to do a ministry that simply does not work with marriage. They are not Joe Accountant who serves on the church's missions committee or Susie Schoolteacher who helps with an after-school inner-city children's program. I'm not saying that those ministries aren't worthwhile, just that they do not preclude marriage in order to advance the kingdom of God. They do not show the requisite kind of calling to be legitimately single.

In addition, these individuals who are legitimately single have been "bridled by the grace of God." When God calls us to do something, he also equips us. In this instance, those who are legitimately single have the gift of chastity—a special enabling given by God to remove their otherwise natural sexual desires. This is why Paul in 1 Corinthians 7:7 acknowledged that he "wish[ed]" that other men were like him in being able to harness their natural sexual desires; but he also acknowledged that having sexual desire is a gift from God.

The Matthew 19 passage teaches us two things. First, it is okay to be unhappy about being single. Jesus said, "Not everyone can receive this saying" (Matthew 19:11). In other words, if we clearly see that we don't fall within these three categories, we don't have to feel guilty for wanting to marry, nor should we feel guilty for admitting we are sexual beings, hard-wired to have and like sex.

The second thing this passage teaches us is that being single is no license to remain single. To be legitimately single requires specific instruction from God. This means that those who are single by personal choice rather than by God's instruction are without biblical excuse for being single. I believe this includes an extremely large portion of Christian young (and not so young) men today, especially since it is within their power to lead a relationship into marriage. On a smaller scale, I also believe it includes women who unnecessarily frustrate the romantic approaches of sincere and honorable men.

SINGLES IN THE BIBLE

All of the single characters in the Bible back up the point of this chapter—that marriage is the rule, and singleness the exception by express calling. Out of the many thousands of people featured in the Bible, only a handful are single: Jeremiah, Paul, Barnabas, and John the Baptist. (We've already mentioned Jesus.)

God told Jeremiah early in his career that he would remain single and would prophesy to Israel. "The word of the LORD came to me: 'You shall not take a wife, nor shall you have sons or daughters in this place'" (Jeremiah 16:1-2). Not all of the prophets were single. Ezekiel wasn't. Isaiah wasn't. Hosea wasn't. Jeremiah was single because *God specifically told him not to marry*. "Before I formed you in the womb I knew you, and before you were born I consecrated you; I appointed you a prophet to the nations" (Jeremiah 1:5).

The idea of being set apart or consecrated is used again in Acts 13:2 when Paul and Barnabas are "set apart . . . for the work to which I [God] have called them." In Romans 1:1 we see that Paul was clear on his assignment from God: "Paul, a servant of Christ Jesus, called to be an apostle, set apart for the gospel of God. . . ." Earlier, in Acts, we read about Paul: "He is a chosen instrument of mine to carry my name before the Gentiles and kings and the children of Israel. For I will show him how much he must suffer for the sake of my name" (Acts 9:15-16). Both Paul and Barnabas led lives of such sacrifice and suffering—thirty-nine lashes at different times, shipwrecked on occasion, imprisoned twice—that being married would have proved extremely difficult, and even detrimental to God's express calling.

John the Baptist's life also conforms to this pattern. Isaiah foretold his coming: "A voice cries: 'In the wilderness prepare the way of the LORD'" (Isaiah 40:3). John knew his mission from the womb and leapt for joy inside his mother when Mary approached, pregnant with his Savior (Luke 1:41, 44). As an adult living out his calling, John was clear about his assignment from God (John 1:23; 3:27-30).

Some people point to the household of Mary, Martha, and Lazarus in Scripture, reasoning that Christian roommating is equal to marriage and family. Roommates are great; don't get me wrong. Roommates can become best friends who remain faithful through all seasons of life. But the point of this book is to make sure we hold to the ideal of marriage set forth in the Bible and don't settle for less than what God wants for us, his children.

Since Mary, Martha, and Lazarus are in the Bible, what do we learn from them? First, while it does mention the fact that these three siblings lived together, Scripture doesn't exalt it. Even in that day this would have been an odd living arrangement. Their ages are not given, and the most we can assume is that their parents were deceased. Their status isn't highlighted in the Bible as an example to follow—it's just a statement of how it was. It can no more be used as a pattern to justify singleness than it can be used to deny the benefits of marriage.

Jesus spent time with them in their home, but nowhere does Jesus demonstrate any kind of open-ended endorsement for their alternative living pattern, nor does he applaud singleness, especially in light of his own words found in Matthew 19. And despite the fact that both of these sisters spent time with Jesus, listening to his teaching, Martha still accused Mary of being unhelpful and not doing her part around the house (see Luke 10:39-40). It could be that their unusual household was somewhat unstructured and that it was hard to know who played what role and bore what responsibility.

I believe that living with roommates—creating a pseudo-family situation—often throws familial thinking off-kilter. There's always one roommate who arrives with the toilet paper and milk for that week and wants a certificate of accomplishment. Hardly will a man and wife ever go through the rituals of detailing who does what—both assume that they are working together for their common good.

Despite all this, roommates are often seen as the answer to a single woman's woes. My friend Jane went to her pastor to talk about her frustration with being single at thirty-two. She was lonely and unhappy about being single and longed for a husband and children. He listened and told her that a roommate was the perfect answer to her loneliness. She was furious. "How can a roommate fill the void for a husband and family?" she asked. "How am I supposed to 'cleave' to a roommate?" She went on to say that she'd had roommates in the past; while they'd been good friends, they hardly filled that kind of void.

Having a roommate is great for sharing the costs of living; and if friendship happens, that's an extra bonus. But we can't fool ourselves into thinking that a roommate can be a viable substitute for marriage. We have to be careful that a roommate doesn't become a placebo for the spouse-shaped hole God created within us. This is why spinsters often come in pairs. They are clogging up each other's spouse-shaped hole, but not filling it in the way God intended. Moreover, it's not only women who fall into this trap. Think about it—most men today think they do not need women because their lives are already crowded with friends and fun.

PAUL AND "IT'S BETTER TO BE SINGLE"

We can't look at what the Bible says about being single without addressing 1 Corinthians 7 because it is the basis for much of what is taught about singleness within the church today. So let's look at what it has to say—in light of the whole Bible, including what Paul said about marriage elsewhere in the New Testament.

Most singles are under the impression that 1 Corinthians 7 validates singleness. It doesn't. Like Matthew 19, it excuses singleness only for limited reasons. We must examine the passage carefully. Assume that a criminal law textbook has a section on self-defense as a justification for using lethal force. Now assume that same textbook, at the very beginning, establishes that murder is prohibited: "Thou shalt not kill." What if someone read that textbook and came away with the generalized notion that killing must be okay? We would wonder how in the world that conclusion was reached and would immediately correct that person by explaining that killing is justified only in self-defense.

My point is that we currently interpret 1 Corinthians 7 to say that singleness is great and even preferable though the rest of the Bible contradicts that conclusion. We should not view this passage as validating singleness as a way of life but instead as setting forth a qualified exception.

Paul Wrote This in a Context

First Corinthians is a written response to a series of questions posed to Paul regarding a wide range of issues from the Lord's Supper to lawsuits, marriage and divorce, speaking in tongues, and so on.[8] Chapter 7 is Paul's response to a specific inquiry (verse 1 says, "Now concerning the matters about which you wrote"). Since the question is not restated in the letter, we must deduce what was asked by the way the question is answered. It appears that the Corinthians had asked Paul whether a temporary delay of marriage was permissible because of a severe famine in the Greek countryside around A.D. 55. Moreover, Paul also foresaw the persecution of Christians that occurred in A.D. 70. The Corinthians were also wrestling with some ascetic presuppositions that taught the shunning of the physical, temporal world, including marriage, and they wanted to know Paul's take on the ascetics who advocated an austere life of self-denial.

Paul had very different advice for different categories of singles. He began with widows and widowers (v. 8), moved on to those who were married but on the brink of separation or divorce (vv. 10, 15), and then addressed never-married singles (v. 25: "now concerning virgins" [literal translation]). To this last subset, Paul said that "in view of the present distress," those who wished to temporarily delay marriage could do so. What was this "present distress"? Historians uniformly believe that Paul was referencing famine and persecution.[9] In light of such events, marriage and family—especially young children—would only add to the stress. It was only because of the highly unusual circumstances surrounding the Greek countryside that Paul gave this advice to this one group of Christians, wanting to "spare" them "worldly troubles" (v. 28) inevitable to marriage and to help them be free from additional "anxieties" (v. 32). This is also why Paul urged husbands and wives to hold each other and their possessions loosely (vv. 29-31).

As an additional justification, Paul noted that those who remained single during this "short" time (v. 29) would be better able to serve the Lord (cf. v. 33), unimpeded by concerns over what to feed hungry, famine-ridden family members (v. 28: "will have worldly troubles").[10] Paul's advice is limited in time and scope, relating "singleness and marriage to the present crisis."[11] Keeping this in mind, Paul's entire argument is one of "expedien[cy]," "[n]othing farther."[12]

When Paul gave his answer to their question, he allowed that difficulties such as famine and persecution are justifications for *postponing* marriage, but he did not lend any support to ascetics looking for excuses to *shun* marriage. Because Paul wanted to debunk the Greek ascetics, he said three times that if someone does marry, that person has not sinned (1 Corinthians 7:9, 28, 36).[13] Paul walked a fine line, but he did not say that singleness and marriage are equal options in the eyes of the Lord.

Some Modern Bible Translations Miss the Mark

First Corinthians 7:1-2 states, "'It is good for a man not to have sexual relations with a woman.' But because of the temptation to sexual immorality, each man should have his own wife and each woman her own husband." Some modern translations render this "not to marry," but if that were correct, then Paul would be undermining the first three chapters of

Genesis, where God, the one who gave Paul his apostolic authority, stated that marriage was good because it was "not good that the man should be alone." Commentator Simon Kistemaker says that this questionable translation of 1 Corinthians 7:1 "misses the mark" and that the translation of the first sentence should be, "It is not good for a man to touch a woman," with the term "to touch" being a euphemism for fornication.[14] In fact, Paul himself asserted a right to take a wife (1 Corinthians 9:5). Similarly, in another letter of the Bible Paul advised younger widows to remarry and not be idle busybodies (1 Timothy 5:13-14).

Remember, Scripture does not contradict itself. Therefore, a contextual, whole reading leaves the impression that Paul was not advocating singleness in 1 Corinthians 7 but was informing the Corinthian congregation that marriage is God's gracious provision for adults to have a sexual outlet and protect themselves from Satan's schemes (1 Corinthians 7:1-9).

Paul Agreed with the Genesis Mandate for Marriage and Sex

Kistemaker also points out:

> Paul . . . fully understands . . . God [created] . . . Adam and Eve and their descendants with sexual needs that are met through conjugal union in matrimony. . . . [A]nyone who has not received the gift of continence but tries to exercise restraint experiences undue emotional distress. In addition, this person also faces a spiritual problem of carrying the burden of sin and guilt for his or her incontinence.
>
> When sexual needs are met in marriage as God prescribes, a person usually lives a balanced life full of joy and happiness and is free from guilt or remorse over sexual sins. Conclusively, Paul endorses matrimony and instructs people who lack self-restraint to enjoy the sexual satisfaction marital life affords.[15]

Commentator Gordon Fee points out:

> Most interpreters read . . . [Paul's] clear preference . . . for singleness, as a wish [vv. 8-9] on his part that people did not have to get married

at all. In light of the argument . . . it is much more likely that he is referring to his actual gift of celibacy, which would mean celibacy in its true
sense—not referring to singleness as such (after all, many who are
"celibate" in this sense wish they were otherwise), but to that singular
gift of freedom from desire or need of sexual fulfillment that made it
possible for him to live without marriage in the first place.[16]

Paul himself "qualifies [singleness] in terms of spiritual gifts"[17]
(1 Corinthians 7:8-9). Simply put, Fee concludes, "[C]elibacy is for the
celibate."[18]

Paul's Advice Was Limited to That Particular Time

In this passage Paul repeatedly explained to his audience that he was
speaking and not the Lord, except in verse 10, when he informed the
reader that he was giving a command of the Lord insofar as divorce was
concerned. But Paul did sometimes tell his readers that he was expressing a personal opinion ("my judgment," vv. 25, 40). He was emphatic in
his declaration that this passage of Scripture did not convey the Lord's
commands regarding marriage and singleness.

Calvin agreed that because what Paul was saying could be "misap-
prehended," Paul wrote "conditionally."[19] Because the "Lord does not in
any part of Scriptures declare . . . persons ought to remain unmarried,
[but] . . . says, that male and female were created together," that is the
reason Paul himself said that he had "no commandment of the Lord."[20]
Because the whole of Scripture "call[s] every one equally and without
exception to marriage, [and since] celibacy is nowhere enjoined upon
any one, or commended," Calvin saw Paul's letter as "giv[ing] advice."[21]
Calvin explained that Paul was drawing upon his apostolic authority not
to set up mandates but to assert that he had more weight than the
ascetics, whose views had contaminated the church.[22] Other modern
commentators agree that the manner in which Paul spoke in
1 Corinthians 7, especially verse 25 and following, is "not your standard
Paul."[23] His counsel only pertained to the advisability of marriage in certain given circumstances.[24]

Fee notes:

One of the unfortunate things that has happened to this text in the church is that the very pastoral concern of Paul that caused him to express himself in this way has been a source of anxiety rather than comfort. Part of the reason for this is that in Western cultures we do not generally live in a time of "present distress." . . . Beyond that, what is often heard is that Paul prefers singleness to marriage, which he [personally] does. But quite in contrast to Paul's own position over against the Corinthians, we often read into that preference that singleness is somehow a superior status. That causes some who do not wish to remain single to become anxious about God's will in their lives.[25]

A RETURN TO BIBLICAL SINGLENESS

In response to all of this, most deliberately single people I have met (people who choose to be single on purpose—usually men) often justify their status by pointing to some sort of pet ministry project on the side. Don't get me wrong—I'm not against ministry projects at all. But people are generally not set apart to singleness to build Habitat homes, serve once a month at the soup kitchen, or take a missions trip for a week or two each year. All those things can be done with a family—in fact, they can even be done with a family in tow.

At the same time, these singles are not ready to give up dating—only its logical end result of marriage. As a single woman, these kinds of men drove me crazy! You simply can't have it both ways. Besides not being fair, Matthew 19 (and God's Word as a whole) doesn't validate this kind of singleness. Neither did Paul, single though he was. You cannot justify protracted singleness on one hand and insist on dating on the other. If you are called to be single, you are called to follow the Bible's counsel on singleness.

The biblical criteria for lifelong singleness are much tougher than what we've tended to follow: The Bible requires voluntarily and permanently renouncing marriage and all that goes with it. As 1 Corinthians 7:37 says, it requires one who "is firmly established in his heart" and is determined to engage in a task that is clearly unaccommodating to family life, a task for the sake of the kingdom of God. If someone were to remain single because he was called to be a missionary in a Middle-

Eastern country where Christians are persecuted and the church operates covertly, he has a good reason for the postponement or avoidance of marriage. The physical safety of one's family is a valid issue. But "I was too busy taking care of my family's business" is not going to measure up against the biblical criteria for legitimate singleness.

Biblical singleness is hard. It requires giving up dating, sex, and marriage and committing to work for God in a sacrificial way. If you're not called to this kind of singleness, you're called to marriage. There's no middle ground. Of course, if you're a single woman but are not called to singleness, it's not usually your fault. You can't get married if no one's asking. But there are some things you can do to change your status (more on that in Part III). For now, rest assured that if you're not called to biblical singleness, you don't have to pretend to like it!

EXCUSES, EXCUSES!

A married woman at church was angry with me for questioning singleness like this. As we talked, I learned that she was actually angry because she had two unmarried sisters. She understood the Bible and could see its clear teaching on the subject, but when it came to her own family, she was unwilling to give Scripture its due. She insisted that her sisters were exempt from marriage because their elderly parents had not saved up for retirement and needed their support. I totally agreed that what the sisters did was noble and good. It is definitely God's will for Christians to care for and support family members. But I wanted to know where in Scripture we are given that exception from the rule of marriage.

There is no such exception. The exceptions are clearly outlined in Matthew 19, and her sisters just didn't meet the criteria. If she'd been honest and said that no decent men had ever asked her sisters to marry, I could believe that. That's certainly not a justification for remaining single, but it is certainly a plausible explanation for why her sisters, and most women today, are not married.

There is something very wrong when we as Christians are not willing to abide by what Scripture mandates and instead insist that our personal circumstances are sufficient for excusing us from what the Bible says. God has said, "I am the LORD your God, who teaches you to profit, who leads you in the way you should go" (Isaiah 48:17). To assume that we know better than God is a dangerous proposition.

Calvin believed that one of the "[tricks] of Satan [to] dishonor marriage" was to advance "the pestilential law of celibacy."[26] In plain English, the belief that remaining single is legitimate and godly is a work of the devil. Read that again: Satan dishonors marriage by fooling us into believing that singleness is okay.

That sounds extreme, I know. But it makes sense. Why break up a home through divorce or wayward children if it is easier for Satan to convince singles that they have no biblical duty to pair up in the first place and that other arrangements are suitable substitutes? Calvin wrote:

> Many think that celibacy conduces to their advantage and therefore, abstain from marriage, lest they should be miserable. . . . [H]eathen writers [have] defined that to be a happy life which is passed without a wife . . . [and they] attempt to render hallowed wedlock both hateful and infamous. To these wicked suggestions of Satan let the faithful learn to oppose this declaration of God, by which he ordains the conjugal life for man, not to his destruction, but to his salvation.[27]

Calvin lived about 450 years ago, but not much has changed. Instead of "heathen writers" insert "television and movie producers" or even "certain ministers" and it works just as well. Pick up a magazine, turn on the TV, or go see a movie: Singleness is fun! Look out for yourself, have a good time, and do whatever you want whenever you want. Get married and you'll get trapped. Listen to many sermons on singleness— it is often exalted almost to the point where you wonder why the minister himself bothered to get married.

THE WHOLE TRUTH

I was talking to a friend who is getting closer and closer to forty, is still single, and is tired of it. "I agree with this," she said. "I see that God designed marriage as the norm. I'm not called to be single in any of the ways Jesus talked about. But it's not my fault that I'm still single!"

I agreed with her wholeheartedly! Most single Christian women today are not at fault for having to endure protracted singleness. We live in a world where it is most often men who pursue and propose. After all, how many women do you know who got down on one knee and popped the question? Not many, I'd wager. Many people quickly point to Feminism and say that women are frustrating men. But the truth is that most single Christian women hardly resemble that caricature.

The average Christian single woman isn't at fault here. (At the same time, we're not powerless. There's a lot we can do—keep reading!) But just because we're faultless does not mean we can use the Word of God to give protracted singleness legitimacy. Whether we are deliberately single or single by default does not serve as a basis for biblical excuse.

"Great, I was already feeling bad enough being single. Now you tell me that my status has no biblical legitimacy," you protest. "Thanks for cheering me up, Debbie."

I know, I know. I've been there. But putting the idea that protracted singleness has no biblical legitimacy on the table is vitally important and can only help us all in the long run. We can't let our emotions about how an idea makes us feel cloud our search for the truth. (And remember what Jesus said about truth: "you will know the truth, and the truth will set you free," John 8:32.)

The thesis of this book is not new—there was a time when every Christian believed it. Past generations viewed singleness as a social deviancy (not the norm), and that had consequences. Men did what was expected and believed to be normal—they pursued marriage. Isn't this what single women want today—to be married?

As single Christian women, we must ask for the truth, the whole truth, and nothing but the truth on singleness—not validation and affirmation for something we don't really like in the first place. As a culture, we must return to God's Word and recapture some of the older, more responsible truths on how to view and treat singleness. We must declare outright that singleness in general is not biblically supported—without clamoring that we feel personally attacked.

When this old idea is new again, single men will feel the pinch to behave in more biblically masculine ways and to pursue wives in a more godly and timely fashion. Only then will we see the dawn of a new day, with the real promise of marriage rather than the false comfort of flattery.

CHAPTER 3

Historical Views on Marriage and Singleness

Single women often feel stuck and are likely to believe they are personally at fault for being single. My friend Rebecca—a beautiful blonde, blue-eyed girl with an amazing voice, from a good Christian family—always blamed herself for her unwanted singleness. She used to point to other women and say, "I can understand she's married, but not me." "If I could just shed this extra five pounds." "If I only had a more promising career." But she wasn't overweight or unintelligent. She was cute and had a Master's degree and a meaningful job. I hated to see her blame herself and wanted her to consider if her singleness could be the result of something else. Could it be the system?

I shared what I was learning with her and told her that the reason we were husbandless had very little to do with us. There wasn't much to separate us from single women in the 1960s or the 1730s or 500 B.C. Just like them, we wanted husbands who would love and care for us. We wanted a bunch of little ones who would tug at our skirts and sing in the children's choir. Our advanced educational degrees hardly differentiated us because those women had their work and so did we. Even Deborah, seen in the Bible as one of Israel's judges, had a husband. So, what had changed?

What had changed was how society viewed marriage and singleness, and how uniformly past cultures agreed on the mandate for marriage. What had changed was how seriously families took on the responsibility to see their daughters married. What had changed was the formality with which the marriage search was launched versus the chaotic informality of today. What had changed was that we no longer lived in a culture where marriage was prized, and we were paying the consequences. What had changed was that we no longer agreed on an objective definition of marriage.

The discussion that began with Rebecca years ago continues today. I want you to evaluate where we were and where we are now and how we can return to Eden, so to speak. For this discussion we must acknowledge that Scripture is the basis for all knowledge and wisdom. This is why the two chapters you just read are critical. Without an understanding of what Scripture says about marriage, its intended purpose, its universal application, and its ever-so-limited exception of singleness, we lack a framework to examine whether past cultures were correct in what they believed about marriage.

MARRIAGE WAS CONSIDERED A DUTY

Throughout the ages, almost all cultures have believed that marriage was the rule and singleness a rare exception. In particular, the church adhered to the position that the Bible both *commended* and *commanded* marriage.[1] The church commended marriage as a worthwhile goal to achieve, a state holding value above all others, and commanded marriage as a necessary part of adulthood.

Marriage was defined as a permanent union of two mentally fit and able-bodied people—one man and one woman—for life. This union had two purposes: mutual comfort and producing the next generation. John Witte, author of *From Sacrament to Contract*, states, "The duty of marriage stems from God's command that the man and woman unite, help each other, beget children, and raise them as God's servants."[2]

Marriage was an expected part of life and the benchmark of reaching adulthood. It was a firm conviction among the Reformers that "all persons should heed the duty and accept the gift of marriage—for the sake of both society and each person within it."[3] Martin Luther, in his famous sermon "The Estate of Marriage"(1523), said:

[A]fter God had made them male and female, he blessed them and said to them, "Be fruitful and multiply" [Genesis 1:28]. From this passage we may be assured that man and woman *should* and *must* come together in order to multiply. . . . Hence, as it is not within my power not to be a man, so it is not my prerogative to be without a woman. Again, as it is not in your power not to be a woman, so it is not your prerogative to be without a man. For it is not a matter of free choice or decision but a natural and necessary thing, that whatever is a man *must have* a woman and whatever is a woman *must have* a man. . . .

"Be fruitful and multiply" . . . is more than a command, namely a divine ordinance which it is not our prerogative to hinder or ignore. Rather, it is just as necessary as the fact that I am a man, and more necessary than sleeping and waking, eating and drinking and emptying the bowels and bladder. It is a nature and disposition just as innate as the organs involved in it. Therefore, just as God does not command anyone to be a man or woman but creates them the way they have to be, so he does not command them to multiply but creates them so that they have to multiply. And wherever men try to resist this, it remains irresistible nonetheless and goes its way through fornication, adultery, and secret sins, for *this is a matter of nature and not of choice.*[4]

John Calvin echoed these sentiments, saying that the "choice to marry is not put in our own hands, as if we were to deliberate on the matter."[5] He considered those who willfully rejected marriage to be "carefree" and "foolish."[6]

Past Christians acknowledged that God created men and women in a very specific way to fulfill specific commands, and therefore their very natures would make them seek marriage as the *only* viable solution to fulfill those commands. Today we view marriage as one option among many.

Dr. Albert Mohler agrees that even within the church we have lost our understanding that marriage is a duty imposed on all of mankind. He remarks:

According to the Bible, marriage is not primarily about our self-esteem and personal fulfillment, nor is it just one lifestyle option among others. The Bible is clear in presenting a picture of marriage that . . . [t]he man and the woman are made for each other and the institution of marriage is given to humanity as both opportunity and obligation. . . .

[T]he Bible assumes that marriage is normative for human beings. The responsibilities, duties, and joys of marriage are presented as matters of spiritual significance. From a Christian perspective, marriage must never be seen as a mere human invention—an option for those who choose such a high level of commitment—for it is an arena in which God's glory is displayed in the right ordering of the man and the woman, and their glad reception of all that marriage means, gives, and requires.

Clearly, something has gone badly wrong in our understanding of marriage. This is not only reflected in much of the conversation and literature about marriage found in the secular world, but in many Christian circles as well. The undermining of marriage—or at least its reduction to something less than the biblical concept—is also evident in the way many Christians marry, and in the way others fail to marry.[7]

In our Western minds, we have an almost caricatured understanding of marriages in the past. We believe they were arranged like impersonal business transactions and were loveless, and that women were treated as chattel in the exchange between families. C. S. Lewis used the term "chronological snobbery" to describe our feelings of superiority when we glance back at the past.[8]

But we must ask ourselves some basic questions when we examine those who preceded us in time. In all of the previous generations that married before us, did women really do so holding up their noses? "Well, I wanted brawny, but hey, brainy is close enough." "I really wanted to marry that doctor, but the plumber Mom and Dad picked out rules!" "I wanted to marry for 'love,' but the money and financial security aren't bad."

Were women having their romantic hopes dashed and marrying unwillingly, waiting to pounce on the opportunity to repeat the same doom for their daughters? For the thousands of years that marriage has been around, were women being told to shut up and marry until late twentieth-century do-gooders freed them from paternalism run amuck? Our modern sentiments about the past are less than accurate, to say the least.

Some readers may balk at the idea of marriage as a "duty" and assume that I am advocating that people enter marriage without love.

That could not be farther from the truth. In fact, that is not what past Christians advocated either. Romantic love was not seen as a threat or competitor to fulfilling one's duty. In fact, it was considered a complement because it would cement a union.

Despite their reputation as sexually repressed prudes, the Puritans celebrated romantic love and, yes, sex.[9] Sex was seen as a "God-implanted natural or biological appetite," and more than just a physical act, for it involved the totality of two bodies—their wills, emotions, and souls.[10] Like the Anglicans, the Puritans did not consider romantic unions the wayward by-product of "affectionate individualism," for it was a pairing of both body and soul. The Reformers too did not believe that anyone should be forced to enter marriage. They actually executed fines, and even imprisonment, on parents if the consent of their children upon entering a marriage had not been freely given.[11]

There Was a Right Time to Marry

Marriage was considered a duty in the past—and one that had a specific time frame to follow.

Accepted in 1647, the Larger Catechism of the Westminster Confession said this about marriage and singleness:

Q. 138: What are the duties required in the Seventh Commandment?
A. The duties required in the seventh commandment are [among other things pertaining to holiness of mind and body] . . . marriage by those that have not the gift of continency. . . .
Q. 139: What are the sins forbidden in the Seventh Commandment?
A. The sins forbidden in the seventh commandment, besides the neglect of the duties required, are adultery, fornication, rape, incest, sodomy, and all unnatural lusts; . . . prohibiting of lawful, and dispensing with unlawful marriages; . . . entangling vows of single life, *undue delay of marriage* . . . either in ourselves or others.[12]

These answers to the Catechism questions reveal that past generations of Christians believed that singles were under a biblical obligation to marry and that deliberately delaying marriage was a sin.

The Bible supports this conclusion and prescribes a right time for marriage. The phrase "wife of your youth" or "bridegroom of your youth" is often used in connection with marriage (Proverbs 5:18; Malachi 2:14-15; Joel 1:8). But what does "youth" mean? It refers to a time when two people (a man and a woman) ought to be prepared to marry and to be given in marriage. Biologically this refers to a time when the two are relatively young and can make the most of their sexuality and their childbearing years. The term means the spring of one's life, as opposed to the summer, fall, or winter. The term "youth" denotes a time when all the rights and privileges associated with marriage can be enjoyed.

While some women have wonderful stories to share about how they met Mr. Dreamboat at forty-three, we cannot suggest biblically ethical frameworks based on individual circumstances alone. Other than the obvious decrease in fertility, loneliness, and exposure to sexual exploitation, there are some real opportunity costs when one marries too late (we'll look at those costs in more detail in Chapter 7).

My point in writing this book is to resurrect this duty as found in Christian antiquity. Duties inform us of what is expected and affix our responsibilities. Thus duties also affix blame when they are spurned or grossly neglected. If the duty is once again touted with the same force as that expressed in classical Christianity, then those who are in a position to execute it (i.e., the men) are more likely than not to follow through. Instead of taking this duty to marry at a specific time as a personal affront and reminder of failure, let's embrace it and ask for a return to a Christian worldview that believed in this duty to marry and held responsible those who failed to execute it. The older order of things held far more promise for women, for it saw women as vulnerable, had compassion for them, and shamed men who abandoned their duty of timely marriage.

Marriage Had Greater Value than Singleness

Marriage was long believed to produce positive spiritual growth and development that singleness was simply incapable of accomplishing. The Reformers (both Lutherans and Calvinists) agreed with their Catholic counterparts that marriage had positive spiritual benefits that singleness did not, and both elevated the character of marriage to a "direct expression and result of redemption and salvation."[13] The Puritans saw marriage as benefiting "man's natural and spiritual life," and spouses were exhorted to look at each other "not for their own ends, but to be better fitted for God's service and bring them nearer to God."[14]

The view that marriage was a blessing was common. Thomas Becon, an Anglican divine who wrote with as much force and passion as Luther and Calvin, found that celibacy commended or commanded by the church would not only cause "abominable whoredome," it would lead to a "sorrowful and uncomfortable" single life, for it would quash man's natural desire to seek out comfort, joy, and help from another.[15] Marriage was considered the "best estate," created by God to set forth the glory of himself, nature, and man, so the "number of [the] chosen people of God [would] be fulfilled."[16] Puritan Robert Croftes wrote that God had "indulgently provided against man's loneliness" through what he called "wedded leisures."[17] Marriage was seen as far superior to a life of loneliness.

William Gouge echoed these sentiments, and in *Of Domesticall Duties* he wrote:

> ¶27. Of marriage and single life compared together.
>
> Let now the admirers and praisers of the single estate bring forth all reasons, and put them in the other scale against marriage. If these two be duly poised, and rightly weighed, we shall find the single life too light to be compared with honest marriage. All that can be said for the single estate is grounded upon accidental occasions. Saint Paul, who of all the pen-men of holy Scripture hath spoken most for it, draws all his commendations to the head of Expediency, and refrains all unto present necessity.[18]

Anglican Jeremy Taylor wrote in "The Marriage Right (or The Mysteriousness and Duties of Marriage)" that in limited circumstances during the early days of the church

> . . . it pleased God . . . to inspire [in some a] strong desire to live a single life; because the dissemination of the gospel required poverty and

martyrdom, the single life was advantageous. But after that storm was over, the state of marriage and family returned to its first blessing, as that "hallowed" and "to increase and multiply."[19]

Past Christians did not elevate the state of singleness but saw it as one of expediency in very limited circumstances, such as famine or to spread the gospel when travel was very inconvenient. They understood that the nature of man included his sexual nature, which could only be satisfied through marital sex. They believed that legitimate singleness happened only "one in a million" times and that adults in general were under the original creation ordinance to be fruitful and multiply.

Today we have been taught the exact opposite—that singleness is great and is equal to marriage. And we wonder why so many people are stymied in their search for a spouse!

PAST CULTURES SHAMED SINGLENESS

Past Christian cultures shamed improper singleness. They considered married life as "far more excellent than the condition of the single life."[20] They also believed that the covenant had to be successfully transferred from generation to generation. Hence, many of the older statutory laws mandated male leadership in the home and expressed the belief that "God ordained man to live in families."[21]

In our earliest American settlements, local ordinances were passed to have "stray bachelors and maids under the discipline of a real family governor" immediately upon their arrival from other shores.[22] Historians Susan Kellogg and Steve Mintz report that new immigrants, and sometimes convicts, were housed with reputable families so that "disorders could be prevented and ill weeds nipt."[23] Singles were required to live with established families, and they enforced laws against single men living alone.

Take the case of John Littleale of Haverhill, Massachusetts, who was found to be living "in a house by himself contrary to the laws of the country, whereby he is subject to much sin and iniquity, which ordinarily are the consequences of a solitary life."[24] He was told to find a real family to live with or the court would help him find one. And if he refused? They'd be only too happy to place him in a "house of corrections." That's right, jail!

Early Americans did not think the single status or life anything to be glorified, but rather something that a "real" family should absorb, so that no one would have to suffer the infirmities of singleness, nor its vices. They wanted to restrict the negative consequences associated with singleness—loneliness and the anonymity needed for the continuation of secret sin. I suspect that the Puritan living patterns not only emanated to the surrounding public what was normative but also had the effect of limiting the choices of single men, with marriage being the most viable option. A young man like single John would much rather quickly grow up and take a wife so he could be king of his own castle than be treated as an immature child in another man's domain.

Even as late as the 1960s, the bachelor was considered a "freak of nature—an adult who was no adult and a child who was no child."[25] The "selection of a mate" and "adjustments" to marriage were signs of healthy adulthood; the "bachelor was viewed as a child—selfish, immature, and possibly suffering from a mother-fixation."[26] Shame was regularly given against the "perennial bachelor," and words like *carefree* and *eccentric* were associated with his status. These were not terms of endearment but of derision; these men had failed in their societal duties. Society didn't indulge single men with a presumption of innocence, believing that a myriad of reasonable explanations could exist for their singleness. Instead it judged the carefree bachelor lifestyle as lacking in both values and character. It judged him to be a man who couldn't prove his manliness.

With women, the labels were somewhat different. *Spinster* had and still has a negative connotation and was generally directed at those women whose fiercely independent spirits drove off potential suitors. Most of society usually employed the term *old maid* for single women who appeared to be past their prime for marriage. It was a term that embodied pity, for she, unlike the spinster, had not frustrated her future but was a victim of poor opportunities for marriage.

Today we neither have contempt for young men who are chronically single, nor do we have the kindness to have pity for young women. We pretend that somehow both are "gifted for singleness" and that neither sex is to blame.

MARRIAGE WAS SERIOUS BUSINESS

What most dramatically separates us today from cultures in the past is that they *actively* advanced marriage for young people. Today we believe that marriages just—poof!—passively happen as planets align and fate steps in. Past societies were different; they believed in actively scouting for potential spouses. Parents looked for potential candidates for their children to ensure the continuation of the family line and believed that their children's full potential as human beings would not be realized without marriage. The Puritans were key in developing a higher standard for parental duty: Parents could consider their duty done only when their children were established in their callings with good husbands and wives.[27] Parents were expected to be proactive in the lives of their children not only by preparing them for the marketplace, but also by preparing them to be good husbands and wives and mothers and fathers in the next generation.[28]

Other parts of society also assisted singles into marriage. Christian charities existed to spare women from "spinsterhood." These charities stepped in to provide for poor women who had no dowries when one was required, allowing them to get married.[29] Luther rescued dozens of women from cloisters[30] who were put there by families lacking funds to keep them any longer. He then arranged for many of their marriages. One such "nun" was his own wife, Katherine. After she foiled three of his attempts to marry her off, Luther finally relented and realized her designs for him, and the rest is history. Past cultures believed marriage was important for women and their personal well-being. Women were surrounded by those who not only supported their innate desire to be married but actually advanced that agenda.

Because marriage was not an optional part of life, it was taken seriously, and most societies organized themselves so that the pursuit of marriage was conducted in a timely, efficient, and, most importantly, protected environment. Parents guided their children to select mates based on familial parity in societal standing, financial backing, and other cultural commonalities. Because most societies believed that, left to their own devices, men would be overcome by their baser instincts, life was set up to make men both want and need marriage in order to have a civilized life. Women were largely unavailable outside of marriage, and men were required to work hard to win a woman's hand in marriage.

Because these former cultures limited and guarded access to women, men were forced to grow up, be mature and financially stable, and make responsible, wise, and efficient decisions. Men today have virtually unchecked access for unlimited amounts of time, and this often produces complacency and generally unwise behavior. How hard we search for an object usually shows its value. A missing shirt button might merit a glance at the floor. But when a wedding ring is involved, the whole room will be turned upside down. The generally aimless, thoughtless, and disorganized practice of dating to find a wife is closer to looking for the cheap button than the invaluable wedding ring. Because we as a culture no longer value marriage, dating is treated as casually as we ultimately treat our marriages. People do not date seriously because they do not value marriage seriously. Bad habits are hard to break.

Marriage Was a Public Institution

Christians in the past believed that the civil good of any society was dependent upon each generation's repeating the marriage mandate.[31] They believed that God had ordered mankind to live in families, and each generation was required to pass on a biblical understanding of marriage and family to the next generation.[32]

The civil and statutory laws in those societies strengthened and supported the institution of marriage and its purposes: mutual love, procreation, and protection from lust.[33] Marriages that did not meet the above stated goals were simply not allowed.

For example, sexual dysfunction, frigidity, or being a eunuch would have been automatic disqualifications for entering marriage. The older order of things would not have allowed such a marriage to take place because procreation was seen as an essential component. The DINK ("double income, no kids") households we know of today when couples marry and live only for themselves would have been considered an anathema of sorts. While procreation is not the sole goal of marriage, these older cultures understood it to be an essential component and believed marriage to be the "nursery of heaven."[34] Similarly, in Calvinist Geneva the marriage of a significantly older woman and a younger man was not permitted, being seen as "contrary to the laws of nature" since their union would not produce children. Understanding the nature of sexual temptation, both Calvinist Geneva and the Puritans in this country had laws mandating that a couple marry within three to six weeks of announcing their engagement. Adultery was punishable by death, and premarital sex involved the stigma of wearing a lettered veil at the eventual marriage ceremony—or even criminal sanctions in some cases. Divorce was virtually unknown, and unions could not be dissolved lightly.[35]

Laws allowed engagements to be dissolved for "staleness." In Calvinist Geneva, a young man who strung a young woman along for years was made to appear for criminal sanctions.[36] Today we all have at least one good friend who has dated a guy for years and still has no ring on her finger. She is faced with the quandary of whether to throw more "good time" after "bad" to see if her time, emotional, and probably physical investment will pay off. She has no claims on him, and there will be no reprisal, stigma, or negative measures assessed against him for squandering her time if he leaves so late in the game.

Past Christian cultures upheld that marriage had to meet an objective definition: It had to be entered into seriously and permanently for mutual society, help, comfort, and children. These concepts were intertwined in the biblical ethics on marriage as a duty. Christians of the past did not believe in privatized marriage-making.

So, what happened? A radical change of thought occurred during the Enlightenment, a period following the 1700s when the "reason of man" was thought to be more profound than the revealed wisdom of God. In *From Sacrament to Contract*, John Witte, Jr. notes that the ethic of the family that was virtually uniform between Catholics and Protestants in past centuries was set aside.[37] Enlightenment reasoning held that "The terms of the marital bargain were not preset by God or nature, church or state, tradition or community. . . . Couples should now be able to make their own marital beds, and lie in them or leave them as they saw fit."[38]

The Enlightenment agenda did not come without debate, and its opponents at that time feared that when marriage became a private affair between the couple without the oversight of parents, the church, and the state, the "inevitable [result would] expose women to great abuse."[39]

James Fitzjames Stephens prophetically declared that changing marriage to contract theory and rearranging society would be inequitable to women, leaving them maimed in their effort to strike "equal" bargains in finding a mate.[40]

The full impact of Enlightenment thinking really did not show its ugly face until the end of the twentieth century, when the American family experienced every form of assault from skyrocketing divorce, illegitimacy, abortion, homosexuality, premarital and extramarital sex, and cohabitation. It is primarily in the last generation that we have felt the net effect of Enlightenment thought in undermining much of what was "sacred in the Western legal tradition of marriage."[41]

Even as late as 1970, most marriages were intact, young women got married around their early twenties, and protracted singleness was rare. In the 1960s a college-educated woman in her late twenties or early thirties and still single would have represented a minuscule 1.6 percent of all women ages twenty-five to thirty-four. In the entire country that amounted to 185,000 women. Today college-educated singles make up 28 percent of all women ages twenty-five to thirty-four, and their population is 2.3 million.[42]

Just one generation ago society still valued marriage. Today we don't. That society still believed in the permanency of marriage, and their statutory laws reflected the seriousness of marriage. Today our laws don't. The gradual acceptance of Enlightenment thinking resulted in liberalizing the divorce laws from fault-based to "no-fault" statutes. Divorces, which once took an act of the state legislature to grant, after the 1970s were freely granted for reasons of "irreconcilable differences." No longer are the biblical reasons for adultery or desertion needed, but just a simple, "I don't love you anymore." The divorce rates changed immediately, and by the mid-1980s one in three marriages ended in divorce.

Moreover, even in the 1950s and 1960s, people understood that marriage was for the production of offspring. Whether they knew it or not, they had the Genesis understanding of "be fruitful and multiply." For centuries Protestants and Catholics shared the belief that birth control was wrong. However, the Protestants retreated from this position, making the ban against birth control a uniquely Catholic position. This, of course, led to the question that if a married couple can privately decide their own fertility, why not unmarried couples? In fact, why not let an unmarried woman decide to the exclusion of everyone else? Since *Roe v. Wade* in 1973, women have been freely deciding what to do with unplanned pregnancies, while those men who had their fun are reveling in their now unspoken right to have sex with only minimal consequences, their right to abandon women they once used as their "wives," and their right to be childish, single, and unfettered. When we began to see life as not so valuable, marriage, as the way to produce life, also began to have less value. If we lose our understanding that God intended marriage for the production of children, we lose our understanding that marriage must be entered by a certain time in order to fulfill that purpose.

Lastly, the modern school of Feminism has not helped women either. The promise that feminists made in advocating no-fault divorce laws was that it would free women. Instead it has left single mothers with children the poorest segment of society. Instead of playing up the female virtue of chastity, they taught women not to be better women but to adopt negative characteristics normally attributed to men, such as sexual roaming. They promoted the belief that men and women are the same—that men and women have the same needs, operate in the same manner, and have the same amount of bargaining power. (I am not talking about the *equality* of men and women before their Maker; I am talking about *sameness*.) But there is no sameness because we were made "male and female." Men do not bear and carry children; women do. Because Feminism goaded women to exercise sexual freedom prior to marriage, the distinct stages of dating and marriage began to run together.

Prior to this time, marriage was meant to represent a greater level of commitment and intimacy. But with the sexual revolution, sexual intimacy could be had without commitment, and this doused some of the male impetus toward marriage. Consequently, today it is not only adults who have premarital sex; studies indicate that more than 75 percent of young people in America have had sexual intercourse by the age of nineteen. Women used to leave home to marry and live with their husbands. Now an interim period exists when people live alone or in peer groups or cohabitate with someone of the opposite sex (something that was previously practiced only among the very poor, often referred to as "shacking up").[43]

These sweeping changes affecting single women today happened mostly in our lifetime and affect how we approach love, marriage, and singleness. Singleness is now inoculated from criticism. If the institution of marriage can be entered into lightly and dissolved lightly, then whether one defers entering into marriage or delays marriage due to self-indulgence or never enters marriage at all become decisions that can hardly be criticized.

THE CHURCH HAS CHANGED TOO

For the church, the playing out of Enlightenment philosophy meant that the two-parent family was no longer the typical model. On the simple basis of grace and compassion the church has accepted these changes.[44] Much of the contemporary church believes that there is "no ideal form for the Christian family," and that it should not be "for or against any particular form of the family or for who ought to be living together and for how long."[45] We now prefer more amorphous concepts, with *family* defined as "everyone is a brother or sister and the family is the family of God."[46] In essence, many modern mainline churches have adopted a strategy of accommodation over classical biblical thinking.

In this brave new world, the church is often paralyzed by the fear of offending divorced people, childless couples, single parents, blended families, and singles. As one social scientist put it, "[Our] rhetoric of inclusion for family diversity obscures the social and moral consequences of family breakdown for children. . . . [W]orr[ied] about provoking debate and dissent in their churches, [ministers] don't even attempt to articulate [biblical] teaching on marriage and divorce."[47] The "unwilling[ness] to confront the cultural and social forces that undercut marriage"[48] carries over in how we treat singles with the same misguided compassion. This accommodation over classical biblical thinking causes the church to affirm singleness instead of challenging whether any of them should be single.

Protracted singleness has no accountability when the church accommodates everyone and everything. The church is in danger of becoming a rubber-stamping machine for virtually all kinds of behavior that previous generations of Christians thought wayward. When neighboring churches easily accept divorced people without researching or directing fault, it sends a message to the community that marriage is not serious business. When marriages are no longer serious business, then it becomes pretty easy to convince singles into believing that they are gifted by status alone, without examining fault, sexual escapades, immaturity, foolishness, or self-centeredness. There can be no accusation of timeliness because each person gets to make up the rules as they go along. There can be no deviancy where there are no standards.

The church today must acknowledge that its present posture overthrows commonly held, centuries-old Christian ethics. Infected with "enlightened" thinking, the church is no longer advocating the duty to marry or that the timely and godly expression of sexuality for procreation must be considered. When the standard is defined downward or is confused, no one ever has to feel any shame about his or her status, nor does anyone have any incentive to press on toward more Christian behavior.

CONCLUDING THOUGHTS

In all of this, there has been a giant paradigm shift. First, there is no longer an equal distribution of power to bring about a marriage. In the past, a woman had every resource behind her to tame young men into wanting marriage. Her family members, those who were beholden to her through blood relation, helped her toward marriage. Today that power has been transferred to the hands of young men—to pursue or not pursue her based upon their own timetables. Do you see what has happened? The person who was sometimes the least reliable and least trustworthy in the marriage equation has now been given the primary responsibility in bringing marriage about.

Though many a woman believes that her personal preferences to choose men have increased, the truth is that her unguarded availability actually decreases her chances and choices to marry. Men usually fail to make wise decisions when they believe their choices are unlimited; instead they often make no decision at all. In the end, both sexes are the losers.

Second, a woman enjoyed a cultural and legal infrastructure that supported and encouraged her desire to marry. The law protected the permanency of marriage and thereby upheld its seriousness. Culturally, her family members and church members took an active interest in seeing her married; they even devised ways to spare her from spinsterhood. Today forget any sympathy for being single, but be prepared for a lecture on contentment.

Our beliefs about marriage have changed radically over time. Seeing this shift in thinking will help as we move into Part II to examine all we've been taught about singleness and marriage. But first let's examine the lack of male leadership we face today.

CHAPTER 4

The Lack of Male Leadership:

THE TRUE CAUSE OF PROTRACTED SINGLENESS

Think about the last beer commercial you saw on television. It probably went something like this: *A group of men in their early thirties sit at a bar watching football, yelling and cheering like a bunch of teenagers. There are no women in sight except for the beautiful waitress bringing them beer and smiling at their schoolboy antics.*

Now think about the last car commercial you saw: *A bunch of men in their late twenties pile into an SUV and head up a mountain with all kinds of "toys" packed in the back and on the roof. There are no children, no wives, no families. It's just the guys out having fun together.*

Men are rarely pictured with wives and families (unless it's a mini-van commercial!). Instead, what's being sold is a life of fun and freedom; men are encouraged to pursue their own happiness and to extend their adolescence as long as possible.

The most popular sitcoms convey the same message to men. Consider *Seinfeld, Friends,* and even *Everybody Loves Raymond.* Have fun, live for the moment, don't answer to anyone, and always leave your options open.

In *Seinfeld,* two out of the three lead male characters are virtually always unemployed. Kramer has no job and is depicted as an eccentric man who blows in and out like a storm. George goes through job after job and often makes up phony careers to impress women. He often lives at home with his parents. Despite his inherent handicap of job instability and short, stocky, bald looks, he still somehow manages to believe that he is in a superior bargaining position and has something meaningful to offer women. Jerry, though gainfully employed, exemplifies the perennial, picky bachelor who for trivial reasons ruins relationship after relationship in the quest for the perfect woman. Both George and Jerry are relieved when their respective engagements fail to materialize into marriages.

In *Friends*, Joey and Chandler are perennial bachelors constantly searching for sex in short-term relationships and for fun in front of their televisions and video games. Ross, who apparently is searching for true love and marriage, has suffered three divorces by the end of the show's run. While Chandler did marry, it's not hard for viewers to come away with the impression that marriage is irrelevant and the better way to go is hook-ups and unlimited freedom.

In *Everybody Loves Raymond,* the roles of two of the leading male characters are anything but reflections of leadership. In both households the women are completely in charge, seem to make all of the heavy decisions, set the tone for the direction of their respective families, and as a result have nothing but contempt for their husbands.

As our culture has shifted to balance power and roles between men and women, there's been a widespread result among men. Since men's maturity and adulthood is no longer measured by taking a wife and starting a family, men have been given the freedom not to grow up and pursue the things that accompany adulthood—namely, a wife and family. Men have been given license to have a protracted adolescence. In today's culture men are encouraged to look out for number one and to be the kids they always wanted to be—without their parents saying no, and with the financial freedom they've achieved.

Most of the men I observed on the dating scene were essentially boys in men's clothing. I remember one guy (we'll call him Steve) who had amazingly managed to get a girl to agree to marry him. Steve's comments about his upcoming wedding and marriage were fascinating to me. He started with, "She'd better not tell me how much I can hunt and how much I can spend on my hunting gear." It went on from there. I marveled because his statements spoke volumes on how he viewed marriage—as some sort of union where two people live under one roof and have legitimate sex, each doing their own thing without the approval or consent of the other. There was no concept of "submitting to one another" in love (Ephesians 5:21), which is the biblical hallmark for the deep, abiding love that Scripture prescribes for the marriage relationship, so that the two are one (Genesis 2:24). He didn't want oneness with his wife; he wanted to be a law unto himself.

But not all men I came across were this way. Take my friend Pepper. He and I along with several other lawyers went to Universal Studios, Orlando for a day of celebration following our duties of monitoring the post-election fiasco in Florida in 2000. Determined to go on every thrilling ride, we begged Pepper to go on one such roller coaster. His response was fascinating: "I can't. I have a bad back. And if I do anything here to unnecessarily injure it further, I will have to answer to Cindy." He certainly wasn't physically scared of his wife, for he had twelve inches and a hundred pounds on her. What Pepper showed was a willingness to sacrifice fun for his family and their need for a healthy dad and husband. Pepper understood that he and Cindy had to be on the same page regarding every facet of their lives.

Steve and Pepper represent two entirely different views when it comes to marriage. Unfortunately the Steves seem to be winning. Why are so many men living their second childhoods, hanging out with the guys, rather than getting married and taking their kids to Little League? I believe there are three main factors behind the dearth of leaders: an education system that allows and promotes indefinite schooling, a lack of leadership in the home, and a lack of leadership within the church.

All too often, Christians are quick to fix blame on the feminists for the problem of protracted singleness. But if we're going to look at marriage and why so many people are stuck in singleness instead of getting married, we have to take an honest look at the lack of male leadership today. Don't get me wrong—I like men. I even married one! But leadership is primarily given to men in the Bible, whether fathers, pastors, or even single men. God called the man Adam to account first.

THE BOGIE OF FEMINISM

The argument against Feminism goes like this: *Feminists produced easy sex, and therefore marriages aren't happening now.* Almost fifty years ago C. S. Lewis remarked on the plight of the late twentieth-century woman:

> A society in which conjugal infidelity is tolerated must always be in the long run a society adverse to women. Women, whatever a few male songs and satires may say to the contrary, are more naturally monogamous than men; it is a biological necessity. Where promiscuity [in general society] prevails, they will therefore always be more often the victims than the culprits. Also, domestic happiness is more necessary to them than to us. And the quality by which they most easily hold a man, their beauty, decreases every year after they have come to maturity, but this does not happen to [a man]. . . . Thus in the ruthless war of promiscuity, women are at a double disadvantage. They play for high stakes and are also more likely to lose. I have no sympathy with moralists who frown at the increasing crudity of female provocativeness, these signs of desperate competition fill me with pity.[1]

When we point to Feminism as the cause for singleness, we show our own hypocrisy. If indeed easy sex has deterred single men from marriage, then we need to concede that today's Christian single man is not celibate but is probably a sexually satisfied single. On that basis, why do we insist that 1 Corinthians 7 gives single men some kind of biblical exception to be single? Why aren't these presumably overly sexed single men being disciplined by the church, or even excommunicated for failure to repent for engaging in a sexual outlet other than marriage? Pointing to feminists and easy sex is a convenient distraction from the real problem concerning the formation of Christian marriages. Blaming feminist theory is as untenable as pretending that Adam's silence and lack of leadership had nothing to do with the Fall.

As parents, as a culture, we have failed to develop a large number of marriage-material men. Many men say they would love to be married, but the greater question is, should any woman have them? Most of them are lagging behind the women in this culture. Compared to women, fewer men go to college today. Fewer men save up and buy houses. Many men today are like overgrown children who live for themselves and then right at the cusp of forty or some other mystical age according to their internal male alarm clock, they try to acquire a wife, if at all. Instead of battling feminist ideology that very few Christian women buy in the first place, we must call men on the carpet and ask them to be the leaders that God made them to be. We must not get stuck battling the bogie of Feminism.

It's like we want to focus attention on and criticize the efforts of fire-fighters to put out a blaze but never look at what started it. If firefighters get burned, we think they probably should have expected it, perhaps even deserved it. After all, they chose to be in the business of dealing with fires. Unfortunately, this is the same attitude facing women. We think women today deserve to be single for choices they made, like attending college or buying a house. How dare they be successful and leave men behind? As if one sex's success prevents the other's.

EDUCATION AND INDEPENDENCE

In Western culture, we often equate a woman's lack of economic need to be married to a desire of not wanting to be married. There is an unspoken axiom that if a woman pursued a high-level, fairly sophisticated degree, somehow she shot herself in the foot and now deserves to be single. Inwardly we want women to be punished for getting higher education and having their acts together. I have heard people in the church say that when women take the lead, men retreat, pointing to Genesis and the actions of Eve. We have it backwards. When men sit in silence and forgo leadership, women start doing things. Adam was in the garden with Eve, had been given headship over her, watched the entire conversation (with a talking snake!), and yet did nothing. No intervention, no "Stop talking with that animal!" It's like he sat back, popped open a beer, and then when everything went to pot complained, "The woman you gave me . . ."

Education is hardly the same thing as taking over the headship of a man. In Asian cultures, women have far more scientific and even "manly" technical degrees than their white American counterparts. Yet in the old Orient (not under commercial Western influences, unlike

Japan) or in India, these women are not suffering protracted singleness; instead, their degrees make them more viable candidates in formal marriage searches. Education is an asset there and is treated as such. It is only in this country that Asians also suffer belated marriage-making and in fact marry on the average a bit later than their white collegiate counterparts. This supports my point that our Western culture and our mating structure, not educated women, are hostile to marriage.

In the church and in the culture we think a woman's advanced degree implicitly tells men to retreat, and therefore she deserves to be single. We mistakenly think that if a woman has her affairs in order, she is sending off signs of independence. We vilify her instead of complimenting her for industriousness and intelligence.

Just because women now have careers in virtually every field does not mean they want the independence of being single. Women often have no choice but to prepare themselves to be market competitors because they cannot rely upon men to marry them, or for that matter to stay married to them.

Most men interviewed on this subject today say they prefer independent women who can carry their own weight. Men, in general, do not want women to be dependent. The social science research in this area shows that "[m]en expect women they date to be economically independent and able to 'take care of themselves.'"[2] This proves that women are not leaving hapless suitors in a dusty haze due to obsessive career development goals. This proves that most men today want a "pay your own way" type of deal where the mantle of adult responsibilities of assuming the care of another is avoided and their personal autonomy remains unchecked. This allows many men to keep jobs that resemble hobbies and to maintain hobbies as costly as their jobs. The convenient scapegoat of Feminism obscures the discussion of leadership and accountability.

THE PERENNIAL STUDENT

My husband had a long-time friend who, despite his stellar accomplishments in high school, decided to pursue his first leg of higher education at the local community college. Somewhere along the way he dropped out and got a full-time job and decided to finish a degree at a technical/trade school. Every semester for three years we would check up on his friend, and it always seemed he was three credits or one class shy of graduating. Finally, unbeknownst to him, the school credited a class and informed him that he was graduating. He was almost thirty.

He was beside himself—not with happiness, but with the fear of what to do next. All this time my husband and I had been encouraging him to find a wife and get married. He told us that he wanted to continue his education by applying for another degree, this time in philosophy. We responded with disbelief and told him that if he wanted to learn philosophy, he could always read a book. Another four years of formal learning would do nothing for his computer career and would have marginal, if not negative, value in preparing him for marriage. He said he was confident that if he pursued additional schooling, his future wife would understand that he needed to do it for his own personal growth and that his extra learning would be of great benefit to his future family and possibly even future Sunday school pupils.

I warned him that women might not be as understanding as he hoped. Many single women would view him as inefficient and irresponsible, an expert at squandering his time and delaying marriage for himself and another. After all, it would be one thing if he had started off with the intention of studying philosophy and finished up by the time he was twenty-two or twenty-four with a Master's degree even, but he would hardly command respect by switching horses so late in life to pursue yet another avenue of personal interest.

This story is not unique. Another young man after four years of college, three more years in law school, and a series of short-term, quasi-legal jobs decided that he was really interested in learning history. He asked his girlfriend if she would accompany him to the University of Virginia, where the two could get married, and she could continue practicing law so they would have the resources for him to pursue a Master's degree and then a doctorate in history. They were both in their late twenties, and she told him he didn't have the luxury of pursuing indefinite schooling on "her time and her dime." It would be one thing, she said, if they were eighteen or twenty years old and she agreed to support him so they could start a family by their mid-twenties. But it was just too late in life for him to ask for that kind of a sacrifice because she would not only be postponing starting a family until her mid-thirties, but she had no guarantee that his fickleness would end after getting yet another two more degrees, or that he would eventually take on a real job with real responsibilities.

What these stories prove is that men often do not think they have to live up to any realistic timetable in which they present themselves as marriage-ready—formal schooling completed and gainfully employed. Culture has said it's perfectly acceptable to go to school indefinitely.

Granted, some of this is the result of a defunct public school system that requires people to go through almost four years of college before they attain the same level of knowledge that came with a high school diploma almost a generation ago. And because we have an unprecedented number of people entering college, there is a race to the top, where people feel the need to pursue an unprecedented number of postgraduate degrees to distinguish themselves from what is now considered the average.

The tragedy in all this is that it systematically forces young people to delay marriage. When they do graduate from college, they have increased their monetary debt and spent four years to make themselves market-ready and marriage-ready. (Of course, some people do get married in college, but most don't.) Now couple this with the fact that most students arrive at college with no sense of calling instilled by their families (they have no clue about their gifts and talents to help them hone in on which degree they ought to be pursuing), they take on average five and a half (not four) years to graduate, and graduation from college often only qualifies them to wait tables and return to the parental nest. It's not hard to see why marriage is put on the back burner.

Marriage still could occur much sooner than later. The simple truth is that men (and women) could be marriageable candidates by the time they are twenty-two, as opposed to twenty-seven and twenty-nine, which is now the national average for first-time marriage by college-educated females and males respectively.[3] The college experience can be great for meeting the opposite sex. The only question is whether these men want to pursue women in a fashion that demonstrates leadership, direction, sensibility, and purpose. And for men that does mean settling on a career path early in life so they can afford to take on a wife and family.

THE LACK OF LEADERSHIP IN THE HOME

The lack of male leadership hasn't happened overnight. While many wonderful Christian homes look to Scripture for guidance, over a generation the parent-child model in a vast number of homes in this country has been reduced to an economic arrangement, where home is little more than a daily pit stop. Parents supply economic support and discipline based on convenience. "Not under my roof" is a common refrain. The message is that rules aren't based on objective truths and unchanging standards but on who pays the rent. As a respected pastor/author says, forming a child's soul and steering him into his life's calling have not been as pressing as paying bills and doing laundry and thus were grossly neglected. Parents pretend that children don't have "brains or souls until they have graduated from college. We aim at nothing, and we hit it every time."[4]

When they are finally no longer under their parents' roof, these children switch majors as often as they switch girlfriends and take an inordinate amount of time to graduate. After college they skip from one job to the next, believing that happiness is just around the next corner. Instead of settling on one job or one woman, they keep all their options open. This is the plight of children whose parents don't set goals with them. The parents gave children much without asking much of anything in return.[5] In effect, parents have taught them "hedonism—the seeking of pleasure—before they are eighteen, [and then tried to] turn the tables on them afterwards."[6] As parents considered their own needs greater and showed very few sacrifices, they have in turn taught their children that their "primary preoccupation is themselves."[7] Professor Allan Bloom offers the following observation on our young people:

> This indeterminate or open-ended future and lack of a binding past mean that the souls of young people are in a condition like that of the first men in the state of nature—spiritually unclad, unconnected, isolated, with no inherited or unconditional connection with anything or anyone. They can be anything they want to be, but they have no par-

ticular reason to want to be anything in particular. Not only are they free to decide their place, but they are also free to decide whether they will believe in God or be atheists, or leave their options open by being agnostic; whether they will be straight or gay, or again, keep their options open; whether they will marry and whether they will stay married; whether they will have children—and so on endlessly. There is no necessity, no morality, no social pressure, no sacrifice to be made that militates going in or turning away from any one of these directions, and there are desires pointing toward each, with mutually contradictory arguments to buttress them.[8]

As a result of this open-ended philosophy under which most American children are raised, and because most parents view their struggles with children terminating at eighteen, the end result is that children can be married, but they don't have to be. Marriage, once a rite of passage to adulthood, is now just an option. Marriage used to signify the willingness to take on the responsibility for another human being and offspring. In the past, "[h]ome, not work, was what counted most; without the wife and children at home to work for, work was somewhat pointless."[9] Now parents are satisfied if their children have gainful employment and live on their own.

The elongation of youth is hardly troubling to those in it. It is no longer considered cowardice not to take on responsibility. Many men wish for a return to their collegiate days, preferring to live in an environment requiring little responsibility, maximum autonomy, and few, if any, expectations of family or for family. They want all the pleasures of childhood and the pleasure of being treated like an adult without the pain of adulthood. The very definition of *grown-up* has changed.

[Adulthood used to be described] as a period of "generativity," a period whose primary task is "establishing and guiding the next generation." In a society where marriage has become a "lifestyle choice," and "childbearing" is viewed as the expression of "individual . . . goals" or more generally, of self-fulfillment, it's difficult to recapture how universally human cultures have held to this view. Virtually all human societies have marked the individuals' entrance into this period of generativity through the ceremony of the wedding. Indeed, marriage and adulthood were so intertwined that the wedded state said more about status than chronological age.[10]

Adulthood has gone from something "stable, finished, and prepared to pass on cultural ideals to the next generation" to "fluid, explorative, and uncommitted to any fixed ideas."[11] Thus, "[l]ate marriage is not simply a demographic quirk. The postadolescent is really a kind of freak of culture, an adult who is no adult, a child who is no child."[12] But rarely are parents willing to call their children to task on this.

Unfortunately, Christian parents are often just as guilty as their secular counterparts; they set "low ethical and intellectual standards for [their] children."[13] Parents often compartmentalize between the secular and sacred and do not let Christian thought influence and take over their view of banking, politics, purchases, and romance.[14] Parents who do not transmit a comprehensive biblical view of life must assume that their child will eventually write his own script for life. A much-published author writes about the preferable alternative:

> [Because children] are temporary subjects—good parents are instructed by God to prepare their children to leave at the proper time, in order to establish their own families. Parents bring up their children to be colonists at the proper time, planting families of their own. Consequently, each family is designed to be a culture . . . [to shape and mold the children] according to the standards of the Word of God.[15]

He goes on to say, "God did not create [the child] to stay at home" past a certain age, and it must be anticipated that he is leaving "to form a new primary allegiance."[16] The only problem is that parents are too easily satisfied if the new allegiance is work. Parents spend most of their time preparing children to be market producers and mistakenly believe that if they have children who can "support themselves," they have done their duty.

Christian parents must reclaim God's truth on what a true adult Christian should look like and must rethink whether their present trajectory of parenting will produce adult children equipped to have a lawful calling and settle into the safe harbor of marital life and enjoy their spouse in their youth.

THE LACK OF LEADERSHIP IN THE CHURCH

Undoubtedly, certain changes need to occur within the church body. The primary change is one of thought. The challenge within the church today is to teach people how Scripture really treats and views singleness, instead of how we wish Scripture validated protracted singleness. We must discuss what biblical adulthood looks like, as opposed to biblical manhood and womanhood in some sort of vacuum. We must not assume that we understand singleness better than Christian thinkers of the past.

The church is facing a dilemma. If it sides with Scripture and historical Christianity, standing up to promote marriage and family, it may ruffle some feathers and possibly lose some members. If, on the other hand, the church continues its present teaching on singleness, it faces the same problem. The answers aren't working, and disgruntled singles will know it and search elsewhere.

The answer is not to worry about offense, but for pastors to exercise the biblical leadership granted them and to teach biblically on when and why valid singleness can occur. They must articulate scriptural truth, the whole truth, and nothing but the truth. Sermons on this subject should not be deconstructed to the point that every listener can internalize his or her own personal truth. Evil always "makes its inroads in our personal and social relationships when our moral teaching is ambiguous, i.e. susceptible to multiple interpretations, and confused by misinformation. . . . The crisis highlights the importance of telling the truth in general and the truth about marriage in particular."[17]

The church has no obligation to match-make or start a dating service. That's not the purpose of the church. However, *the church must get out of the way and stop being a stumbling block to the pursuit of marriage.* One minister told parents to not pressure their single children. He cited 1 Corinthians 7 for the proposition that the world "pressured" marriage upon us, but that we are now free under the New Testament to be single.[18] With the rising rates of divorce, fornication, adultery, homosexuality, abortion, and single parenting, what pressure is there to get married? The reason his message was a stumbling block was not only because he mishandled 1 Corinthians 7, but because he undermined parents' doing their biblical duty to see their children enter adulthood through marriage.

Other leaders are proclaiming the truth. One minister is so successful at assisting the members of his singles group toward marriage that he performs weddings almost every weekend. The recipe for his success? He and his wife view these singles as a group of people who should be married because none of them appears to be called by God for singleness. He concluded that the only reason some of these adults were still single was because the men in that group were not taking the leadership to pursue women. Instead of offering excuses or justification, he and his wife take these men aside, have heart-to-hearts with them, and raise them to an acceptable level of marriage material. In other words, this pastor has honed in on the problem and addresses it directly. We need more leaders like him!

The church can gracefully bow out after correct exegesis on biblical passages that are keys for understanding marriage in relation to singleness. Nevertheless, it would not be unbiblical for a church to assist in this manner, as examples of past Christian charities have proved. Having accountability groups for single men to examine their perennial singleness is on par with having accountability groups for other issues that trouble us. But the upshot to this has to be a change in rhetoric on singleness. Until the church returns to preaching the superiority of marriage over singleness and the duty to marry, and until some of these singles (especially the men) start squirming in their seats and feel the shame that is rightfully theirs to bear if they are refusing to follow God's leading into marriage, there will be no substantive improvement in the number of Christian marriages.

Now What?

There has to be a reclaiming of biblical leadership in this country on every level. Leadership requires thoughtfulness, planning, and vision for an intended outcome. It requires thoughtful actions designed to secure an identifiable goal at a reasonable hour. It requires resolve and purposefulness.

As we are surrounded by a lack of male leadership, we're repeatedly told that wishing it were otherwise is pointless. Ask many married women what they want and they'll answer that they want their husbands to lead. This problem is widespread. But there is hope: God created men to be leaders, and he can accomplish this in them. As women, we can partner with God in this work. (More on specific things we can do in Part III.)

Unfortunately, we're often told that to pursue marriage and express our discontent with the single life shows a lack of maturity in our relationship with God. It's time to rethink what we've been taught about singleness and to examine what we've been told in light of the truth of God's Word. In Part II we're going to confront the conflicting messages, emotions, and beliefs about singleness and discover how we can respond biblically and honestly as we move forward toward marriage.

PART 2

Rethinking
THE GIFT OF
Singleness

CHAPTER 5

What We've Been Taught

Suppose a woman showed up at church starving to death, stomach growling, not having eaten for days or weeks. The last thing we'd say is, "Man shall not live by bread alone, but by every word that comes from the mouth of God."

Instead we'd head to the kitchen and whip up something for her to eat. It's not that God can't satisfy us with his Word, but to misuse a perfectly good Bible verse like this could result in death! Starving people need food. Seems pretty simple, doesn't it?

To abuse Scripture in such a way would contradict God's own design as our Creator to satisfy hunger with food. To insist otherwise disregards God as Creator and the one who knows what's best for his creation.

Now suppose someone showed up at church starving for intimacy, beat up from dating, not having heard a specific call from God to be single. Feeling confused, a little angry, and alone, she admits, "I'm hungry for marriage—for a husband and a family."

Sadly, we often refuse to employ the same logic when it comes to the hunger of singleness. Instead of pointing her in a meaningful direction to have that obvious and specific need met, we recommend anything but what's asked for. We often carelessly misuse Scripture to come up with radically inflated, politically correct, feel-good answers for the question of singleness. It's not always an intentional misuse; we are fearful of offense and often shy away from the truth in order to avoid hurting people.

If we sincerely do not believe that God's presence makes up for physical hunger, then why do we often pretend that service activities or God's being the husband of his people makes up for singleness? When we deny that our bodies, souls, and emotions are made for a real marriage here on earth, when we suggest that a real marriage is not that important, or when we suggest that singleness is as honoring to God as marriage, we show contempt for our Creator-designer. Much of today's Christian culture repeatedly informs (or misinforms) Christian singles that marriage is unnecessary, singleness is good, there is no problem with protracted singleness, and singles should be content in their state and embrace it wholeheartedly.

But is this biblically accurate?

From a reading of the previous chapters, we certainly know it is inconsistent with what Christians have historically believed about singleness. The following chapters have been written to show that what we believe today not only goes against traditional Christian teaching on this subject, but it is faulty, unbiblical, and erroneous. Because of the significant departure from Scripture, it leaves the single person high and dry, strapped to an unkind destiny.

BAD ADVICE

Let me recount the story of a man in Northern Virginia after he told his small group that he wanted to get married:

> I was rebuked by the elders because, according to them, the Bible says it is better to be single to serve God better. . . . They, obviously, were married, and I didn't understand, if they felt so strongly about being single, why they themselves weren't single. When I would ask for prayer, I would get a lecture about being content, and was told I needed to stop focusing on self and serve God better. [Three years later, when I was 27, my marital status was the same.] I went to the rail several times seeking God's wisdom on marriage. I was told by the pastor that maybe God wanted me to be single, and that there wasn't much I could do about the situation, other than accept my circumstances. I was told that, if God wanted me to have a relationship with a woman, he would bring this person into my life. The pastor also preached a sermon on singleness, saying that if a person was over 40

and no one had come into his or her life, then this was God's calling
of celibacy.

[The young man then switched churches and began seeking the
counsel of a new set of ministers. But his situation did not improve.]
The first minister I talked to told me that God's plan for my life could
be to be single, and I just needed to accept this. Several years later, I
went for advice to another pastor, who chewed me out in front of several friends for not being open to celibacy. Later, I wrote him again asking for advice, and he wrote back, "Perhaps being single is your
vocation." I went to the senior pastor and he shrugged his shoulders
and said it was too bad, but God doesn't promise everyone a mate. I
was involved in a men's accountability group with two married men.
I expressed my desire to marry. The head of this group said he could
not pray for a wife for me, because he wasn't convinced that I should
be married. I was eventually confronted by two leaders of this group
and told that I was immediately to stop this "whining" about wanting
to get married. When I again raised this issue several years later, I was
told by the leader of the group that he would no longer pray with me
and that I was out of the group.

By this time he was no longer a young man but was nearly forty, and
he decided to join a dating service that then went belly-up after cheat-
ing him out of three hundred dollars. The head of the church's prayer
ministry said, "God allowed this to show him he didn't need the dating
service." Another church member suggested he join a monastery.
Another minister reasoned that since he couldn't get married by now, he
had to accept this call of singleness from God. This man left the church
and now has to talk himself into going to church at all.[1]

When I first heard this story, I was somewhat unsympathetic; as a
man, the ball was in his court to pursue a woman toward marriage. He
really didn't need the help, support, or applause of his church to do
something that was so clearly within his power. But the story stuck with
me because he was surrounded by foolish counselors within the church
body—from leadership to laity—giving him bad, unbiblical advice and
being a stumbling block in his search for a wife.

This story is not unique and unfortunately is not a rare occurrence
in churches today. The messages given to this man over the course of his

single years are typically given to single women also. In her book *The Freedom to Marry*, Ellen Varughese recounts the story of Janet, who when invited to attend a seminar on marriage literally sobbed and cried, "Don't you understand? Jesus is all I need!" Varughese observes, "Janet was a deeply wounded thirty-five-year-old who was desperately trying to believe what she had been taught to believe [i.e., that a single person only needs God, and God alone]. In truth, she was lonely, full of anguish, and not at all fulfilled."[2]

She tells of another woman who asked a minister's wife to pray for her to find a husband but was given the trite response, "I can't pray for you because I don't know if it's God's will for you to be married." The minister's wife was then asked if she were praying for her own daughter. She indignantly replied, "Of course I will pray for her. I know it's God's will for her to get married."

In an interview with Kimberly Hartke, founder of True Love Ministries (a group ministering to those in the throes of protracted singleness), she agreed that church leadership generally sides with the message that singles should surrender their desire for marriage.[3] She shared the story of a woman in church leadership who began outwardly questioning her lack of a spouse and the incompleteness she felt. The moment she suggested to her church that they should reconsider their training "singles to end their love affair with marriage," she was promptly asked to become "content" or leave her position.

Focus on the Family recently approved the Colorado Statement on Biblical Sexual Morality, which states that "[s]exual behavior is moral only within the institution of heterosexual, monogamous marriage" and that "sex outside of marriage is never moral." Fair enough. But they also urged singles to remember:

> God calls some to a life of marriage and others to lifelong celibacy, but his calling to either state is a divine gift worthy of honor and respect. No one is morally compromised by following God's call to either state, and no one can justify opposing a divine call to either state by denying the moral goodness of that state.[4]

It is certainly correct that sexual relations are only legitimate within marriage. However, the statement fails to distinguish between the state of celibacy and the state of singleness. In that document, the single person is taught that celibacy and singleness are the same thing. It also goes so far as to state that singleness and marriage are equally valid options for all people, agreeing with the contemporary church that the state of marriage and the state of singleness are both morally good and acceptable to God. (We're back once more to Jesus' teaching in Matthew 19 and his short list of people who are exempt from the command to marry.)

Today's Teaching in a Nutshell

Well, what do these stories teach us about our beliefs today regarding marriage and singleness? After being single and talking to other singles, here are four key ideas taught to singles. I'm overstating a little, but stick with me:

1. Singleness and marriage are gifts, and both states are divinely equal. There is no way to predict which gift you'll get. Marriage will spontaneously "happen" for some, but not for others. Therefore, you should accept either state without question or complaint. It is beyond your ability to change the situation you find yourself in, and you must assume that God "called" you to singleness. It must be "God's will," so resistance is futile and offensive to God. Because marriage just "happens," you must wait on the Lord until marriage just miraculously "happens" for you. You do not need to search or do anything; God will align the cosmos to bring Mr. Right along at just the right moment. In fact, if you attempt to change your lot, the wrath of God may occur.

2. You must be content with your singleness since you cannot change or control it. Jesus is all you need to be happy; he's the answer to any void or incompleteness you feel. You should be single with great fulfillment, joy, and an absence of loneliness. To be discontent with your single status is sin.

3. God wants you to be single, whether you actually want to be or not. You should keep an open mind about the state of celibacy/singleness because it affords you the much-needed spare time to serve God, something that married people cannot seem to squeeze out for the Almighty. In light of all the service you could do, the pursuit of marriage is essentially selfish.

4. Being single equals being celibate. After all, if you just set your mind to it, you can harness and squelch sexual desire for years or decades until the gift of marriage shows up. Or not. As a single person, you shouldn't struggle with sexual desire. Being single and deferring sexual gratification will not morally compromise you.

In the following chapters, we will carefully examine each of these ideas and see if they can stand up to Scripture. Let's be honest and forthright about our desire to marry. Let's be prepared to give an answer to the catchy (but not very helpful) things we're told as single women today. Let's discover where these ideas came from and how culture has endorsed them, how they mislead us, and what the Bible has to say about them. That way we'll know exactly what to say the next time someone says, "You should stop whining about getting married and just be content with being single."

The good news is that we are not powerless. We can take a stand and challenge these false messages by examining the truth of Scripture and responding with what we learn.

CHAPTER 6

The "Gift" of Singleness and the Sovereignty of God

For years my church had a Wednesday night supper before the weekly prayer service. One night John (not his real name) sat down next to me. As we talked, I asked him if he was seeing anyone special. "No," he said. To me, he'd always appeared a little unsure of himself around women.

"Well," I said, wanting to be helpful, "if there's ever anyone you fancy, I'd be happy to invite the two of you—and some other friends— over for lunch after church one Sunday. That might give you two an opportunity to connect." (My Sunday lunches are pretty fabulous, and I thought he'd be grateful for the offer to include the girl of his dreams.)

"So you think God's working out his will, but you need to help him along?" he replied in a somewhat indignant tone.

After John informed me that his job was to sit back and wait, I immediately retorted, "Do you really think God's will requires you to be inert and not do anything?"

I knew he believed that marriage just spontaneously happens at some indefinite, unpredictable distant time in the future and that "singles, instead of being told about marriage, should be told what they can do as singles." Those are John's words, not mine. Take John's attitude revealed by his words and his action (or lack of it) and fast forward five years. I am married with two little girls. John remains single and has had no dates (from the word on the street) and has no prospect in sight.

Let's look at John's beliefs a little more closely because he is a product of his time and what he's been taught about marriage and single-ness. John, like most singles, has been taught that marriage just happens for some; it's nothing that we do. Because he believes that marriage occurs almost randomly and no one can predict or control it, he has no problem sitting idly by and waiting for marriage to happen to him. Either way John has been told that both marriage and single-ness are gifts, and he accepts either state without much thought or complaint. He will just wait (and wait) and claim that the sovereignty of God is on his side.

Obviously I disagree based on the truth of Scripture and thousands of years of world history. Up until the last thirty years, the cultures that valued marriage didn't just sit back and believe that marriage might happen for people or their children. People actively sought marriage. But not us; we think the first thoughtful action directed at finding a spouse shows that we are circumventing or getting ahead of the Almighty.

Don't get me wrong: I believe wholeheartedly in the sovereignty of God. At the same time I also believe we have free will and a responsibility to pursue God's will for our lives. God's sovereignty doesn't mean we are puppets who cannot take action until he pulls our strings. On the contrary, we are expected to live our lives in ways that follow God's will and do what is right in his eyes. When we misunderstand God's sovereignty, it can become merely an excuse to be lazy and justification for our refusal to assume our God-given roles. We must cooperate with what we know to be God's will for our lives—whether it's loving our neighbors or honoring our parents. Obedience requires action.

Refusing to pursue marriage (something God intended for us unless we fall into one of the exemptions Jesus described in Matthew 19) and sitting back and doing nothing is not resting in God's sovereignty. It is not trusting God. Rather it is refusing to follow his design for our lives.

It's not just John's laziness that's a problem. The bigger issue is that John, like so many others, has been indoctrinated with the idea that sin-gleness is a gift—despite the fact that *no other Christian culture would have supported such a notion.* If singleness is a gift like marriage, and if the two are both morally equal and good, then why pursue marriage?

The first thing to discover is if singleness really is a gift.

Is Singleness a Gift?

I don't know about you, but I love getting presents. I can totally relate to Maria in *The Sound of Music* when she sings that "brown paper packages tied up with string" are one of her "favorite things." There's nothing quite like the excitement of opening up a gift that someone bought with you in mind.

Of course, there are also gifts you're not so excited about. Fortunately, we live in a world of gift receipts, and returning unwanted items isn't hard. Still, there's huge disappointment in opening up a beautifully wrapped package to find the last thing you'd ever want.

So why do we insist that being single is a great gift when it's really the last thing we want? If singleness is such a great gift, why do so many of us hate being single?

Singleness is no gift. That's right. I'll say it again. Singleness is no gift. It is nowhere found in Scripture to be a gift. No other Christian culture considered it to be a gift. Celibacy or the removal of sexual desire in a minority of people is and was considered a gift (see 1 Corinthians 7 and Matthew 19). We have been taught in the modern church that cultural or circumstantial singleness and celibacy are the same thing, but they are not!

The singleness position currently endorsed in the contemporary church is faulty and erroneous. It rests on a huge leap in logic, a *non sequitur*, if you will. It goes like this:

(1) God called some people (a handful) to be single.

(2) He enabled some of them to be single through the gift of celibacy for a task that requires the single life.

(3) Therefore, the rest of the umpteen million single people should not question why they are single but should just trust and wait on the Lord.

Obviously, there are large gaping holes in this understanding. In this case, A plus B does not equal C.

First, why do so many singles hate this supposedly great gift? After thirty years of sermons on being content with being single, there is still discontent. We have been miserable failures in reprogramming singles to end their love affair with marriage.

Second, why are so many singles chronically single? The expectation of marriage and family, which was a birthright for young people in the past, is now accepted as a perpetual game of dating-roulette with high stakes and high losses, few winners and many losers.

Third, in the wake of this cultural war, well over a quarter of the population in the United States is single, when in 1900 only 3 percent of the total adult population was single.[1] Did God just want more gifted singles in this generation? Are singles today just meant to enjoy the gift of singleness longer, or is this generation of singles not meant to enjoy the normal progression of life enjoyed by their forefathers?

Fourth, if singleness and marriage are on equal planes and are equally valid, then whatever happened to the Genesis mandate to "be fruitful and multiply"?

Finally, if Christian singles are gifted, why are their lives as marred as non-Christians? Why have two-thirds of Christian singles thrown away their virginity?[2]

These rhetorical questions should cause the Christian community to consider whether we are using the right paradigm when it comes to singleness. We, the people of God, have willingly gone along with the shift in culture away from marriage and toward long-term singleness and have forgotten our heritage. We've lost our moorings and keep coming up short in our understanding and in resolving the problem of protracted singleness.

A RETURN TO BIBLICAL THINKING

Our present position on singleness is derived from the unholy union of culture, pop psychology, and Scripture. We need to think biblically *first*, then look at culture, not the other way around. Too often we no longer look to Scripture to dictate and serve as the basis for our understanding. Instead we take reality as it exists and then see if we can somehow apply Scripture to it. Placing culture before God's Word has negative consequences for every area of our lives, but when it comes to singleness and marriage, the results are devastating.

If we think biblically first, we are required to bring not only protracted singleness under the Word of God for judgment and scrutiny but everything that precedes it. In other words, we allow the Word of God to do what it's meant to do—to shape how we view protracted singleness, mating patterns, generativity; to shape how we measure biblical adulthood (not just biblical manhood and womanhood in some sort of vacuum); to shape how we view what it means to be created "male and female"; and to shape how we hold people accountable whose behavior falls below the standards set by Scripture. This kind of holistic, biblical thinking forces us to examine whether there is in fact a biblical duty to get married in a timely and responsible fashion in order to enjoy the full rights, benefits, and privileges of marriage.

If, on the other hand, we continue to apply Scripture after the fact, all we do is invent a holy doublespeak of easy answers that adapts itself to the issue. Every status in life (whether temporarily single, married early, married later in life, perpetually single) can be made to look like God's will and therefore above question or examination. "God's will" becomes the blanket answer to any legitimate questioning of the way things are. We can no longer have a discussion of accountability and whether someone's conduct in youthful immaturity for a decade or more resulted in the undue delay of marriage for another individual. Under this backward system, there's no place for the discussion we're having in this book!

Undoubtedly, this backward thinking is circular and less vigorous and assumes a more manageable and tame God. Such mistaken thinking is often more palatable—for the short run anyway. We live under the pressure of modern culture and psychology, demanding tolerance and chiding us for hurt feelings. But if not wanting to cause pain is our motivation for not thinking biblically first, we have truly missed the boat. Protracted singleness is perhaps one of the most hurtful things a single person will have to tolerate during adulthood.

OUTCOME-BASED THEOLOGY

Thinking culturally endorses a seductive, outcome-based theology: Whatever your outcome is—whether you are married or single—it must be God's will. But God is not a puppet, and we should not treat him as such. We must not turn his sovereignty and his will into *carte blanche* approval for the choices we make. Doing so turns the doctrine of God's sovereignty (his control in exercising his will) into a rubber-stamping machine that validates every situation in life, no matter how unbiblical or personally devastating.

This plays out in all kinds of ways. Think about the controversy over homosexuality as a lifestyle. This kind of thinking argues that because people struggle with homosexuality, God must have made them that way on purpose. Because such desire exists, it must be God's will. *Not!*

Or think about what happened in Nazi Germany. One could say that those events were God's will. In a technical sense, those events did happen while God was ruling. But for us to say that God *wills* the murder of six million innocent people completely contradicts what he has revealed in Scripture and inaccurately reflects his desires.

Outcome-based theology affects our view of singleness as well. Current thinking asserts that because so many people are chronically single, God must will it to be that way. Because we apply Scripture after the fact, we accept singleness as the norm, rather than questioning whether the protracted singleness rampant today is biblical in the first place.

Once we accept singleness as the norm, as a wonderful "gift," equal with marriage, it's all too easy to apply Scripture out of context and come up with a view of singleness that God never endorsed. One faulty assumption inevitably leads to another.

Because of the inclination to find seemingly relevant Scripture and apply it out of context, we have been reduced to equating singleness with celibacy, though nowhere does Scripture package the two. Scripture validates celibacy; it does not validate singleness. Even at the outset of 1 Corinthians 7, Paul acknowledged that those who are celibate can be single, but that hardly any singles can be celibate, and therefore he advised marriage (1 Corinthians 7:1-2, 5-6). Paul did not see sexual desire as something to be repressed, something to be put off for the distant future, but as something that should push every man to "have his own wife" (v. 2).

When we automatically equate singleness with celibacy, we assume that singleness can go on indefinitely. But when we look at Scripture, we see that both Paul and Jesus worked under the belief that it is within human power to marry quickly—in our "youth" as Scripture teaches.[3]

Neither one of them was trapped under outcome-based thinking: *If someone gets married in the distant future, then we can conclude that person wasn't called to celibacy.* When we remove our participation in pursuing marriage, we're left with marriage as a waiting game in which we can do nothing but watch for God to drop someone into our lives with a note saying, "I'm the one!"

Singleness is the Result of Choice

If we apply biblical thinking first, we see both marriage and singleness as an outcome of personal, societal, and generational choices and therefore fraught with human mistakes. In that sense the outcome of singleness can be the product of sin—especially cultural sin—without it necessarily being the sin of the person affected.

"Now wait a minute," you say. "I'm not *choosing* to be single. I don't even want to be single!"

I am not suggesting that single women are individually choosing to be single and are therefore personally responsible for being single. What I am suggesting is that other factors are causing them to be single.

For so many women the tragic outcome of indefinite singleness is primarily the product of cultural forces that affect believers and nonbelievers alike—an open-ended, male-friendly mating structure geared toward low commitment, shallow, cyclical relationships as opposed to marriage; a protracted education system that doesn't really educate, containing students who embrace perpetual schooling without any commitment or direction to finding a meaningful calling for the purposes of settling into family life; parenting with only minimal expectations of self-sufficiency; under-involvement of fathers in the lives of their children; the defining down of adulthood and the elongation of youthful adolescence; the lack of male leadership; the removal of societal shame for being a perennial bachelor . . . You get the picture. We no longer have a culture that esteems marriage as a worthy goal, the crowning achievement of one's life. Culturally we think of marriage as optional, and the church agrees, citing God's will as justification for that belief.

Against the backdrop of these systematic impediments, no one is doing the single woman a favor by pointing to the sovereignty of God, refusing to examine these institutional factors and to hold accountable those responsible for her unwanted status. Relabeling singleness as biblically legitimate doesn't work. It would be like a doctor refusing to diagnose or treat cancer, calling the slow progression of decay normal. After all, God could always reverse the cancer. After all, God could always override our cultural deficits and get you married. We have no right to leave a pro-marriage infrastructure, pursue marriage haphazardly (if at all), and then insist that God's mercy and grace make up the difference (and if he doesn't, insist that his will was done).

MISAPPLYING THE SOVEREIGNTY OF GOD

Many singles have been taught that while marriage may show up in the future, it's God's will to be single for the moment. This is said in order to make people feel okay. This is definitely better than being programmed to stamp out your innate desire to marry. The problem is that telling single people they might *eventually* marry doesn't really help because marrying late can mean missing out on what I call the full rights and benefits of marriage.

God has revealed through Scripture that the best time to marry is in our "youth" (Malachi 2:15), not at some arbitrary point in the future. Women miss out on a lot when they marry too late in life: legitimate sex, the protection and caring of a husband, and possibly even children.

Citing providence is not particularly hopeful because it again demonstrates circular reasoning and our willingness to use good theology to dismiss bad cultural behavior. It is entirely too cheap to use faulty thinking or theology to dismiss someone's unintended outcome of being an unwilling single as God's will.

My goal in this book is to confront such hard questions instead of ducking behind the shield of providence. Can we really continue to ignore biblical teaching and the heritage of biblical marriage practices and expect God to pick up the pieces when things go wrong? I don't think so. We must take responsibility for the individual, societal, generational, and cultural choices that have shaped our current standing.

Yes, it's going to be hard to stand up against what's accepted. It's never easy to challenge the status quo. But this system we've accepted is still in its infancy compared with the whole of history, and it's not too late to turn back. Just as we are living with the results of the choices made by those who've gone before us, we can change the future for those coming next.

A QUESTION OF GENERATIONAL SIN

Let me say again that I wholeheartedly accept the sovereignty of God. I am keenly aware that there is no such thing as a rogue molecule in this entire universe. I know he does not take his eyes off us for an instant.

My question is not one of doubt in his sovereignty or his ability to rule and intervene in our lives. My question is, *will* he intervene—or perhaps, *should* he—given the very deliberate move away from his plan for marriage in the last few generations? Many in the previous generation have failed to assist our generation in terms of biblical wisdom and guidance to accomplish the marriage mandate.

In Scripture, forgetting the past or failing to hand knowledge to the next generation is called sin (Deuteronomy 6:7). It is past generational sin that has kept this generation from attaining marriage.

It is a deeply ingrained rule in the Bible that the sins of forefathers are often visited on children and that sometimes a group of people, or even an entire nation, has to suffer for the mistakes of those who came before them. (Think about Israel wandering in the desert for forty years after the ten spies said they couldn't do what God had promised.)

It's worth asking if the protracted singleness we're suffering from is the result of generational and cultural sin. Do we suffer from interminable singleness? Do marriages often resemble roommating more than the unity described in Scripture? Do so many Christian marriages end in divorce because of sin?

God has certainly operated through generational justice in the past. Why shouldn't he do so today? After all, judgment often comes in the form of getting exactly what you want (Romans 1:24). In this case, previous generations insisted that marriage as God intended wasn't what they wanted; they preferred independence and freedom. They wanted marriage to resemble something they privately wrought. Is it any wonder that single women today are not finding marriage as God wants for them?

93

DEALING WITH THE CONSEQUENCES OF FREE WILL/SIN

God has no obligation to intervene and override the results of our sin. One of the best examples I've found to illustrate this point exists in the black culture in America today. Many black women believe that a large portion of their male community is unreliable and untrustworthy. On average 52 percent of African-American men are high-school dropouts, and black men in their early thirties are nearly twice as likely to have prison records (22 percent) than Bachelor's degrees (12 percent).[4] So what does this mean for these women?

Because black women are not incarcerated in the same numbers as black men (and acknowledging that interracial marriages are rare), many black women will remain unmarried—whether they choose singleness or are single by default. The situation is compounded when these women have children outside of marriage, creating single-parent households in which there is no male leadership. Their sons grow up without a strong male role model and often end up being the kinds of men black women call unreliable and untrustworthy. Thus the cycle continues.

Are black women suffering singleness as a result of their culture? Yes. Are they also compounding the problem with their own sin? Yes. Is God able to intervene and provide a worthy husband for every one of these women? Of course. Will he? Probably not. There comes a time when God takes his hands off and lets us deal with the consequences we've brought about (Romans 1:24-28).

When I've used this example in the past, I've often been dismissed by people in white churches who say I'm comparing apples and oranges. It is the logic behind the example that I'm highlighting here, not the particulars. We don't operate within a vacuum—both culture and individual choice have gotten us to where we are today. God has ordered the world with natural consequences. He can intervene, but he is not obligated to do so.

As another example, look at China after one generation of its one-child-per-family policy. Because many retirement-concerned families aborted female fetuses, the resulting shortage of adult women will cost many Chinese men a wife. The ending of a line is equated in Scripture with God's judgment.[5] Pinning the blame on Communist philosophy alone cannot remove the responsibility due to an entire nation that did not vigilantly protect its natural rights. In other words, the situation in China today is the result of both the government and its people.

Sad outcomes like this are the result of free will—something that occurs under the umbrella of God's sovereignty. I know it's been done to death, but consider the question of bad things happening to good people.

Are the bad things that happen to us God's will? Are abuse, illness, death, and the myriad other things that we suffer in this life his will? It depends on how you define God's will—his revealed will, his necessary will, his preceptive will, his sovereign will. If each one of these different subtypes of God's will are equated with one another in a catch-all concept, then the term *God's will* starts to justify collective human actions that undercut God's revealed will. God does not contradict himself, and he cannot be mocked.

He rules and he overrules every single event in the course of redemptive history. It's not like God is running around trying to put out brush fires. But that does not mean that everything that happens is God's decreed will, though everything that happens does so under his sovereign will since he ultimately works all things for his glory and for our good (Romans 8:28). Consequently, not everything that happens is good. His working all things for good is not dependent upon all things being good. It's not that God doesn't allow bad things to happen. The problem is that glibly calling bad things God's will without qualification makes it look like God himself has authored the bad thing. If God's will is not clearly defined and used correctly in our examination of historical and cultural events, we basically murder the truth, dismiss injustices that God would want us to speak up about, and make God look bad in the process.

GOD HAS ALLOWED SINGLENESS

Often single women are told that God has allowed singleness and that his knowledge and control over the situation should still any troubled heart. In a sense, singles are chastised for pondering why they are not married. I am afraid the analysis of the situation is not quite that simple.

While cancer is regularly allowed into people's lives, researchers still ask what causes and cures it. We don't tell those with cancer, "It's just God's will for you to be sick right now; so you need to be content." It's one thing to trust God's sovereignty in the face of an unknown such as cancer. It's quite another to claim his sovereignty when something's cause is clear. We do not fully know what causes cancer; if we would just open our eyes, we would know what causes the modern phenomenon of protracted singleness.

Marriage should be the culmination of our wise choices based on godly wisdom taught by our parents. Marriage is within our control if we would quit shooting ourselves in the foot and embrace the wisdom that has stood the test of time.

Of course, marriage is ultimately under God's control. But he demands our thoughtful and timely participation in his will. While the farmer praises God for a bountiful crop, he must still plant, water, weed, and harvest. While God feeds the birds of the air as Jesus said, he doesn't drop worms into their nests. They have to go out and search for them. We must cooperate with God's will for our lives rather than sitting idly by and complaining because God didn't magically provide.

Misunderstanding God's will by having a cultural rather than a biblical mind-set has resulted in faulty teaching about singleness. In the following chapters we're going to look at some of those specific messages about singleness from a biblical perspective. Are what we've accepted as answers to singleness really answers? And if not, what can we say in response?

CHAPTER 7

"Wait on the Lord"

If you've been single for very long, chances are pretty good you've been told to "wait on the Lord" when it comes to marriage. Isaiah 40:31 promises that those who wait on the Lord will have their strength renewed. Overall, waiting—not rushing—seems like a good idea. But how applicable is this to the legitimate expectation of marriage? Does God really seek indefinite waiting on the part of single women to get married? Does God really seek unlimited patience in waiting for Mr. Right to appear?

If you ask most singles, waiting doesn't seem so bad at first.

Caroline is twenty-two and finishing college. She expects to get married someday, but there are some things she wants to do first: finish school, backpack across Europe next summer, experience more of what life has to offer. At this point, being single doesn't bother her too much—she's accepted the theory that you have to kiss some frogs before finding a prince. So waiting on the Lord isn't all that hard.

At the same time, she's a little concerned. Her older sister is twenty-seven and still waiting, with no sound of wedding bells in the near future. *Just how long am I supposed to wait?* she wonders. *Five more years? Seven? Ten?*

Michelle has been told to wait for marriage since college. At thirty-seven, she's also wondering just how long she's supposed to wait. "I've never been one to sit around and wait for life to happen to me," she says. "I'm not sure how doing nothing is getting me any closer to marriage and having my own family."

She went on to say, "I don't feel called to be single. I want to be married. I've been taught to 'run the race to win the prize' when it comes to the rest of God's plan for my life. Why not for marriage?"

Exactly.

THE HIGH COST OF WAITING

Undoubtedly there is pressure in today's culture to spare everyone's feelings and to demand tolerance of just about everything. But we cannot use the excuse of "I don't want to hurt anyone's feelings" to refuse to think biblically about this issue. I've said it before: The hurt of protracted singleness far outweighs hurt feelings from the truth.

The notion of waiting on the Lord for marriage often goes hand in hand with the insistence that doing so develops patience. But is patience really a virtue when it delays God's revealed will for us? Because God created marriage with the command to "be fruitful and multiply," there is an obvious time constraint placed on marriage. It becomes harder to fulfill the purpose of marriage the longer you wait.

There is something disturbing about patience that comes with a heavy price tag, especially for women, who by God's design cannot have children past a certain age. It's one thing to insist that an eighteen-year-old have some patience in getting married; it's quite another to say that to the same woman at thirty-five.

Without doubt, the story of the woman who narrowly manages to marry before the age of forty is more a grim reminder of a society gone awry than of the good providence of God. This woman will not enjoy the full benefits of marriage. Aside from reduced or no fertility and all that goes with it, she has had to live without sex for the past twenty-plus years (we hope she did anyway). A prominent researcher in this area, Barbara Dafoe Whitehead, says this woman has faced "prolonged exposure to the vicissitudes of love."[1]

In other words, she may have to be a stepmother to children who aren't hers, or perhaps she can have children, but her older husband has already had a vasectomy. She may very well be marrying a divorced man who will spend half of his income supporting his existing family rather than the family she wanted to have. The idea of "drink[ing]

Libby ♡ ♡ ♡

Don't let life get
you down,
keep being you!
Yes, change & grow
in Jesus
but don't stop being
SPUNKALICIOUS!!
We all make mistakes,
but thank the LORD
for His grace. ☺

Trust Him, & refresh your ♡
with His promises.
I love you, and He loves
you infinitely more!

♡ Porche' Harmony

water from your own cistern" found in the book of Proverbs (5:15) is shot to oblivion the longer we wait to marry. From a completely objective viewpoint, the woman who marries too late will only find a piecemeal marriage.

After seeing *Something's Gotta Give* with Diane Keaton and Jack Nicholson, my friend Bitsy asked me what I thought about it. The movie portrays the romance and love of an older (fifty plus) couple. The big thing I think couples miss out on by marrying later in life is what I call the years of dreaming together, those years when God weaves together the lives of two people to create a common future.

It's like planning your dream home, choosing all the options from doorknobs to light switches, and watching it grow from the pouring of the foundation and the drywall installation to hanging wallpaper and filling it with cherished heirlooms and photographs. The love is more than moving into the house; it's being together every step of the way. When couples marry later in life, many of the steps have been missed.

Bitsy was right that something else was amiss in the movie. Why would a woman want to nurse a man in his old age whose playboy lifestyle prevented her from becoming his wife, lover, and the mother of his children during her youth? Bitsy acknowledged that however we look at it, not marrying early, in our "youth" as the Bible says, has consequences, some of which last a lifetime. The pain of a lifetime of unfulfilled longings doesn't disappear when redefined or when we insist that somehow God was responsible for it.

After reading some of what I've written in this book, a forty-four-year-old single woman was very angry with me. She said that despite everything I've written, she still had hope that she would marry. My response to her was, "So do I." Of course I hoped that she would marry! I hope that everyone not called to singleness will marry. That's why I'm writing this book. My question for this woman, though, was if there had been a cost to remaining single this long. The point wasn't whose fault it was. The point was to be honest about the price she's paid.

Of course, women are not the only ones who suffer. Despite the appealing picture painted on television, men stuck in protracted singleness also have a price to pay. According to Linda Waite and Maggie Gallagher in *The Case for Marriage*, it accounts for a higher rate of criminality and allows men to become more stubborn and often even completely indifferent to the fact that others exist.[2] While some single men may be financially stable and mature, the truth, according to David Popenoe, professor and former social and behavioral sciences dean at Rutgers University, is that "they are so set in their ways that they are lousy at making the compromises that help a marriage get over the rough spots."[3] Just like some single women, some single men will have bouts of fornication on their report cards. And even if they remain sexually pure, staying single confronts them with temptation and a life filled with unspoken and unmet lust.

Protracted singleness teaches men to forgo genuine leadership and to live a life of leisure and convenience, looking out for number one. It becomes all too easy to spend money on immediate gratification (sports cars and video games) rather than thoughtfully planning for a future that includes a family.

The cost of protracted singleness is high for the church and for culture as well. It produces fewer members for the kingdom of heaven than if singles married young and produced more children during their most fertile years. Practically speaking, we have a shrinking or negative birth rate in the West. In order for a population to reproduce itself, the fertility rate must average 2.1 children per woman. The fertility rate today among major developed nations is only 1.6.[4] In America today, over a quarter of the population is single. Some researchers in this area predict that perhaps only 85 percent will ever marry.[5] Because so many single women have had to defer or forgo marriage today, they have decreased fertility and often don't have children.

A Christian commentator observed, "Having fewer people can wreak havoc on an economy, creating both a labor shortage and a shortage of buyers. A government with a shrinking population faces a small military and fewer taxpayers. Dwindling populations have always signaled cultural decline, with less creativity, energy, vitality on every level of society."[6]

Fewer taxpayers in one generation also results in a heavier burden to support retirees in welfare system countries.[7] Due to the negative birth rate in Japan, the legislature there has considered not offering any retirement benefits to older retirement age singles because never-married singles failed to produce children to support and balance the social security scheme in place. We would be shortsighted to think that that kind of measure would not take place in America where the social security system is dependent on each generation's producing enough children to support the generation retiring.

In the Western world, where we could have multiple Christian babies in freedom and raise them safely, we casually dismiss our diminished fertility, while countries like Yemen are producing 7.2 children per woman.[8]

Wait on the Lord/Presume on the Lord

In Elisabeth Elliot's *Quest for Love*, she describes a Christian couple counseled to not act on their mutual attraction for more than six years. In my opinion, this couple basically *wasted* six years, fretting about each other in silence, as if their mutual sacrifice of time would make their marriage better or more pleasing to God. Now while it is certainly not my goal to encourage rushing into marriage, how is it that this couple received "good" Christian counsel to wait that long? How do we know that they would not have been doing God's will by marrying six months or a year after they realized they loved one another? The only thing that story taught was that it's okay to be reckless by not working toward marriage, and somehow God will override their foolishness and get them married anyway.

Instead of moving toward marriage unless God calls us otherwise, single women (and men too) have been taught that it is better to stay single unless God orders marriage. We have it totally backwards! God already ordered marriage in Genesis. *Marriage* is the norm God established from the beginning. *Marriage* is what we're to pursue unless God specifically calls us to remain single.

Remember the earlier story of John? Instead of actively pursuing marriage, he believes his job is to just get on with being single and wait for marriage to fall into his lap. What John was taught and what he is doing is presuming on God. In my mind, it is no different than Satan tempting Jesus to throw himself off the cliff since God had given his angels charge over him. This sin of presumption is hardly discussed in churches today; so John may be unaware that his indolent posture during his single years can contribute to how extended those years become.

It's only been within the past thirty years or so that we as a culture have stopped actively pursuing marriage. We are taught that the first thoughtful action directed toward finding a spouse shows we're bypassing God and refusing to trust in him. We're warned that taking matters into our own hands instead of sitting on them and waiting on God won't end well.

When I realized that I had to take some drastic actions if I intended to get married, I was told that I was behaving like Timothy McVeigh, the Oklahoma City bomber. Apparently McVeigh had cited a poem prior to his execution where he defiantly declared himself to be the captain of his own soul. The inference was that by taking charge of getting married, I also must have thought I was the master of my own life, over and above God.

When singles are told to wait on the Lord, what happens is that people like John become completely inactive. Women not only have to deal with all of the cultural impediments to marriage, but now single men have been made unnecessarily fearful of God's displeasure if they actively search for a wife.

ARE YOU WILLING TO PAY THE PRICE?

Doing nothing when it comes to pursuing marriage will most likely get you just that—nothing. God's not going to drop Mr. Right on your doorstep with a red bow tied around his neck. (Although it's a nice picture, it's pure fiction.)

It's time for us to recognize that marriage is God's will for our lives and begin to pursue what God has in store for us. Passively waiting for what God has declared to be his will can only result in paying a price that is far too high.

When we know what God wants for us, we should pursue it. God made us, and he knows what's best. The benefits of marrying in our youth as he prescribes are years of joy and happiness with one person, building a life together over time. Marriage is wonderful, incredible, amazing! I can't tell you how much I love being married. In marriage I have come home and have found peace, joy, and contentment. There's something immensely satisfying in being completely known by another person. In creating us for marriage, God had something truly divine in mind. When we see something ahead that God has told us is in store for us, let's act like kids on Christmas morning and run as fast as we can to get to what he has prepared!

CHAPTER 8

"Jesus Is All You Need"

"Seeing anyone special?" As a single woman, it seemed like parents, married friends, single friends, coworkers, and the rest of the world were bent on ferreting out every detail of any potential man in my life. Didn't people have anything else to ask me about—my job, my Bible study, the weather?

Especially dismaying was when I had to answer the question with a flat "no." "Seeing anyone special?" was all the worse because it required me to put into words what I already knew—no, I wasn't seeing anyone special, and there wasn't even anyone on the horizon. It always felt like admitting failure, like the lack of "someone special" was somehow my fault.

Though it's a simple yes or no question, it always seemed loaded to me—like a gun that might go off at any second, leaving bloodshed and tears in its aftermath. Of course, I do realize that my friends and family weren't snooping or putting me under the microscope—they were just being nice. Asking the question didn't come from any ulterior motive, just simple curiosity. But I still dreaded hearing it.

As I've listened to friends and acquaintances answer this question, I'm always amazed by women who, instead of just saying no, offer a page-long explanation along with their answer.

"No, I'm not looking for anything significant right now," a woman begins. "I'm really growing in the Lord right now, and I'm so happy/content/secure in my relationship with him. I've started a new Bible study/small group/book club, and my life is so full right now. Being single," she continues, "gives me so much freedom to explore my own interests and pursue friendship/career/ministry. Let me tell you about it in more detail . . . " She runs you through her calendar and to-do list and then pauses. "Of course," she concedes, "I would be open to seeing someone if God chooses to bring someone special into my life."

Chances are you've heard a response like this. While some of us may wonder if it's possible to reach such a place of peaceful acceptance (what I like to call singleness nirvana—that state rumored to be out there somewhere but that doesn't really exist), many of us walk away mumbling, "Oh, come on!" under our breath.

HONEST ANSWERS

Hearing such "holy" responses makes me want to respond that if the freedom, joy, and security of singleness are so great, perhaps she should just forget marriage. After all, why mess up a good thing?

We must be honest with ourselves—and each other—about how we feel about being stuck in protracted singleness if we're ever going to change things. Maybe you're not ready to stand up at the next singles event at church and admit that you've far exceeded the goals of your book club and you're ticked off that you're not having sex. I understand if you're not there yet—few women are ready for such a level of self-disclosure!

When single women tell me how wonderfully happy they are being single, I'm left wondering if they're really trying to convince themselves more than me. When we constantly announce our contentedness, it rings false. The truly content don't need to convince or tell anyone about their contentment.

If single women are so satisfied with their single status, why is there a mad dash for every new singles book offering a new coping strategy? "I can be happy and content being single." "I can do something noble with my life as a single woman." "I don't need a man." "I can increase my knowledge of God."

Am I wrong? Isn't that what virtually all of these books have been saying for the past twenty years? The fact that books selling the idea of singleness contentment abound should speak volumes about the lack of contentment that really exists. Think about it: The fact that so many diet books sell proves that America is fat.

If you are called to true, biblical singleness and are content in your calling, that's one thing. But it's quite another to hide your true feelings about singleness for fear of what people will think.

When I began to research the idea for this book, many women told me in private how many tears they'd shed over their single status. "It's just too painful to pray about my situation anymore," one woman confided. "I've given up hope," said another. Yet another was diagnosed with depression as a result of her unhappiness with being single. Woman after woman confided that they desperately wished to be married but felt trapped and unable to speak up about their need.

Despite living in a fiercely independent culture that values speaking your mind, not one of these women would ever publicly show her need for a spouse or share her desperation. The decision of these women to hide their true feelings is based on more than mere politeness. It reflects their unconscious belief that being a good single person means always being content and putting a glad face on something, even if it's terribly wrong.

We must face our desire instead of running away from it. In talking about desire, author and speaker Ruth Haley Barton says, "In many of us, the fear of not getting what our heart longs for has led us to develop an unconscious pattern of distancing ourselves from our desire in order to avoid the pain of its lack of fulfillment."[1] She goes on to say, "If we don't know how to attend it [desire], we may make the mistake of trying to set it aside or minimize it when instead we need to pay attention to it."[2]

TODAY'S SINGLE WOMAN

University of Chicago professor Leon Kass describes our generation of women this way:

> [M]ost young women strike me as sad, lonely, and confused; hoping for something more. . . . After college . . . women are chronically disappointed in the failure of men "to commit." For the first time in human history, mature women by the tens of thousands live the entire

decade of their twenties—their most fertile years—neither in the homes of their fathers nor in the homes of their husbands: unprotected, lonely, and out of sync with their inborn nature. Some women positively welcome this state of affairs, but most do not. Resenting the personal price they pay for their worldly independence, they nevertheless try to put a good face on things and take refuge in work or feminist ideology. . . . Meanwhile, the bachelor herd continues its youthful prowl, with real life in suspended animation, living out [a] . . . "postmodern postadolescence."[3]

He's hit the nail squarely on the head! He acknowledges the problem facing us today on many levels: the fact that this phenomenon is new and unlike anything in history we've seen thus far; the fact that living in protracted singleness is contrary to our "inborn nature"; the fact that we're often stuck with putting a good spin on a bad thing; the fact that protracted adolescence abounds. One thing, as they say, leads to another.

Kimberly Hartke of True Love Ministries agrees. She states that extended singleness leaves people "debilitated and weary." When asked the direct question of what women were "actually getting" when they do marry at a belated age, she answered that it was a "mixed bag" filled with "sugar daddy wannabes, divorced men" and that a good number of these late-marrying couples would be childless as a result of marrying late in life.[4]

Barbara Dafoe Whitehead, a respected researcher on marriage, family, and singleness issues and co-director of the National Marriage Project, says that the cumulative effect on singles operating in today's system is like "scraping emotional plaque accumulated over a succession of romantic failures and disappointments."[5] Ugh.

Women are waking up to find that feminist ideology has not satisfied their inner woman. In the church we're wondering if the "gift of singleness" theory is really true. The grandiose visions of "dynamic singleness" promised by so many seem to be more fantasy than reality.

As one writer put it, "The reason we are in the current quandary of social, psychological, moral, and spiritual deterioration is precisely because these demagogues have somewhat succeeded in fooling the majority of people to believe in their Peter Pan world, except, as the saying goes, 'You can't fool Mother Nature.'"[6]

God designed us with marriage in mind. We weren't created to live in protracted adolescence, putting off marriage indefinitely. "You can't fool Mother Nature." But stuck in a system that condones such behavior, we're left making the best of a bad situation.

WHAT WE'VE BEEN TOLD

The church has often dismissed the cumulative grief occurring in single women, mistakenly asserting that a greater personal relationship with God will make up for any distress felt over the ongoing single state.

Leaders make the vain promises that "if singles do rest and rejoice in their marriage to Christ, that means they will be able to handle single life without devastating loneliness."[7] Experience proves otherwise.

During the course of my research, a reporter sent me a group of e-mails (with names blackened out) she had received from singles across the country:

> At times, my loneliness makes me long for the release of suicide. At church, the loneliness was most unbearable. I still often wonder what hidden sin I have committed to be denied a family. Relief has only been found within the confines of anti-depressants. . . . I still love Jesus, but definitely feel like a "Child of a Lesser God."

> We singles deal with some very hard issues in our lives that are either never addressed or glossed over with the not-so hidden implication that someone with their act together wouldn't have those problems. Loneliness and sexual temptation are the [two] biggies—Singles are literally dying of lonliness [sic] (at least this one is).

Ministers often inform singles, "Christ is the only spouse that can truly fulfill [singles], and God's family [is] the only family that will truly embrace and satisfy them."[8] How is this even possible? I've been single, and I've been married. There's just no comparison!

I don't believe the church offers anything that can fill that void on a Friday night. It can't make up for sleeping alone, hearing the floor creak and knowing you are all alone. It can't fill the empty space on the other side of the bed. It can't erase that sigh upon entering a dark, empty home night after night because you could only avoid the place for so long as you buried yourself in office work. It can't provide a date for those events designed for couples. It won't send you flowers on Valentine's Day or fill the emptiness on Mother's Day. It doesn't make up for watching nieces and nephews open presents on Christmas morning instead of your own children. It won't make up for the countless microwave meals eaten alone. It doesn't help as you earn wealth and wonder who will inherit it. It doesn't remove that lump in your throat with each passing birthday. It cannot make up for waking up alone for days, weeks, months, years, and decades. There's just no adequate substitute for a husband and family.

Singleness affects every aspect of life. There is nothing that anyone can say, and there's no substitute to make it better. The only solution is to point singles toward marriage in meaningful ways with meaningful prayers. Neither parents, nor siblings, nor church, nor work, nor activities can make up for or do what a spouse is designed to do.

My friend Deborah loved going to church—she went three times a week and said that she'd go every day if the doors were open. Obviously she had a growing relationship with the Lord; she was continually hungry for more of him and his Word. But despite her Christian maturity, she was lonely. She wanted a husband with whom she could share the joy she felt in going to church, worshiping and basking in God's Word.

With or without Jesus, women experience dread as they watch their options for marriage and family steadily decrease with the passage of time. Such a "marriage to Christ" isn't assuaging loneliness within Christian single women or erasing the fact that marriage has been placed just beyond reach.

The feminists falsely claimed that their ideology would set women free, and I believe we have often been equally deceptive within the church. Just as careers and sexual independence left women unfulfilled, so teaching singles to find fulfillment in Christ alone has not erased their loneliness. They have been mistakenly encouraged to believe that God can fill *any* void they might have. "Let Jesus be your all in all," women are glibly told.

We assume that God is so big and powerful that he can fulfill any need, make up for any deficit. We assume that God can fill the spouse-shaped void he created in us. I'm not challenging God's omnipotence in any way. But I am saying that we need to examine whether his own revealed nature would ever make him do such a thing. God's *ability* to do something and God's *willingness* to do that thing are two entirely different things. Just because God can do something doesn't mean he will.

God created us to need food to satisfy hunger, clothing to keep us warm, and shelter to keep us dry. He could satisfy those needs with himself but instead created us to pursue their fulfillment. There is not a shred of evidence in Scripture that God is *willing* to fill the spouse-shaped void with himself.

When we go back to Scripture we see that doing so would go against the very purposes of the "male and female" ordering he established in Genesis. If God had designed man to be solely content in God alone, there would have been no reason to create Eve to be Adam's wife. Before Eve arrived on the scene, Adam and God had undisturbed communion— *it was God who said that it was not good for the man to be alone.* God did not design the vast majority of us to be content without a marriage partner. God designed the spouse-shaped void to be filled by a spouse.

To repeat an illustration, God designed hunger to be satisfied with food, thirst to be satisfied with drink. God created needs to be filled with the very thing we need. Hungry? Eat. Thirsty? Have a drink. Need a husband? Get married!

We're often taught that New Testament Christianity focuses on our individual relationship with Christ; familial thinking was part of the Old Testament way of life and is not applicable to us today, some say. But just because Jesus died on the cross to save us from our sins doesn't mean that our fundamental design as human beings has changed. Our desire for marriage has not been altered by Jesus' death and resurrection. Our design for intimacy and wholeness through marriage remains. We are made in God's own image, "male and female," as his image-bearers, along with our original father and mother, Adam and Eve.

Nowhere in Scripture has God revealed the desire to fill the spouse-shaped void himself or to clog it up with activities, friends, and ministry. The modern teaching that he does this manufactures a false attribute of his character and pastes it onto the God of the Bible. We're thus left with an idol on our hands.

When we protest that this new God, this idol, hasn't filled our desire for a husband, hasn't been all we need, we're charged with having a small God, a lack of faith in God, and not allowing God to be our husband. With this view of God, any time we express dissatisfaction with singleness, we're made to feel that we have an inferior relationship with the Lord.

DISCONTENTMENT WITH SINGLENESS DOES NOT EQUAL SIN

Marjorie once dared to complain to her Bible study that she was tired of being single. There were a few nods of agreement from some of her peers. But the group leader quickly asked her, "How big is your God, Marjorie?" As if somehow it was Marjorie's fault for not appropriating more of this "big God" and as a result being sad with her singleness.

The unspoken message that joy and happiness are good and discontentment and sorrow are bad sends a clear message that we cannot express our frustration with a very real problem. No wonder so many of us put on a happy face, pretending to be fine when we're really crying ourselves to sleep at night!

Somehow we've come up with the idea that the spiritually mature person will experience joy all the time and in every circumstance. By implication, bitterness, sorrow, and unhappiness have become indicators of spiritual immaturity, signs that faith is severely lacking.

This undeclared war on negative emotions is merely another manifestation of the health and wealth gospel that has run amuck. Are you sick? You must not have enough faith that Jesus can heal you. Are you poor? Examine your life for disobedience and get back in line. Are you sad about being single? You must not be trusting God to meet your need for a spouse. No wonder we're surrounded by people who find themselves exclaiming, "No valleys for me, buddy!"

But this is contrary to Scripture. Ecclesiastes records that there is a "time to weep, and a time to laugh; a time to mourn, and a time to dance" (3:4). In fact, the Bible acknowledges a whole range of emotions to choose from.

I'm not saying that we should define reality based on the ebb and flow of our emotions. But Scripture gives us permission to feel sad about being stuck in a situation God never intended—and Scripture also frees us from feeling guilt over that sadness. It's okay to feel miserable about not being married!

It took me almost seven years—seven years!—from the time I entered single adult ministry to admit that I was unhappy being single. I was working so hard to achieve the contentment always just out of reach that I hadn't given myself permission to admit my sadness to myself. How I wish someone had told me in that first year that it was okay for me to be unhappy with my single status! That would have saved me much heartache and energy. Have you noticed how tiring it is to pretend to be fine when you're not?

The only way we can know that we're okay feeling sad about being single is to confront our true emotions and to ensure that they are indeed consistent with biblical truth.

EMOTION IN THE BIBLE

Do we find sadness and desperation in the Bible? You bet. Just take a look at David's raw honesty in the Psalms. He laid it all out before God, never apologizing for his emotions, imploring God to stand true to his word and to arrive with the help David so desperately needed. And David wasn't the only one.

Consider Hezekiah who "wept bitterly" when the prophet Isaiah pronounced his death sentence (Isaiah 38:3). Hezekiah believed that because he had served God faithfully, it was unfair for his life to end so soon. God heard Hezekiah's honest prayer and granted him another fifteen years.

Or consider Jephthah's daughter, who in the face of imminent death, asked her father, "'leave me alone two months, that I may go up and down on the mountains and weep for my virginity, I and my companions' . . . he sent her away for two months, and she departed, she and her companions, and wept for her virginity on the mountains. . . . . And at the end of two months, she returned to her father, who did with her according to his vow that he had made. She had never known a man" (Judges 11:37-39). This young woman was more troubled by the loss of marriage than by her impending death as the result of her father's rash vow. I know I keep coming back to this same idea, but God designed us to want to be married and to act on that desire!

Or better yet consider Naomi, who returned to her country with her daughter-in-law Ruth but minus her husband and two sons. She changed her name to "Mara" ("bitter"). In essence she said, "Call me Bitterness!" (see Ruth 1:20-21). And God did not punish her for this but graciously provided for her and Ruth and proved his love to her.

At least Naomi loved and lost. Today an entire generation of women is asked by the church and is expected by society to behave like widows in the prime of their lives—accepting the fact without bitterness or sorrow that by default they are forgoing the most Creator-blessed relationship this side of heaven.

Because our God is the God of justice, and because he himself has emotions, and because we are made in his image, our sense of justice can be offended by our loss—we sometimes feel sad, angry, and even bitter. To act otherwise when we feel these things is to live a lie!

Back to Naomi. Her bitterness only lasted until her hope was actualized. "Then Naomi took the child and laid him on her lap and became his nurse. And the women of the neighborhood gave him a name, saying, 'A son has been born to Naomi'" (Ruth 4:16-17). Naomi was restored when she held Ruth's baby. When she saw that life would continue, that her family line hadn't died, that it hadn't all been in vain, her life was renewed (Ruth 4:15). Her emptiness was filled.

Naomi didn't have to pretend all was fine when it wasn't. That doesn't mean she never had thoughts about God that she shouldn't have had. But God in his love and grace ministered to her as she honestly acknowledged her pain and sorrow.

Much like Naomi's story in the book of Ruth, the sorrow of protracted singleness is a completely understandable, God-engineered emotion meant to be expressed when this God-ordained relationship is lost or unrealized. Such an emotion is not abnormal or wrong—it's human.

I'm not advocating that we don sackcloth and ashes. I'm not advocating nursing bitterness or sorrow. By allowing bitterness to take root, we allow it to manifest in ugly ways. Feeding our frustration toward men in protracted adolescence can result in the misguided belief that we're better off without them or that we as single women are somehow better than single men.

I am simply stating that sorrow does exist in our hearts as we evaluate the high costs of protracted singleness. The price of long-term singleness is high for women. It produces women who have had to live in a sort of limbo and the possibilities that may go with it—failed relationships, a heartbreak or two, repentant bouts of fornication, cohabitation, unwanted pregnancy, abortion, a doubly-increased chance of being raped without having the protection of a father or husband, strained relationships in substitute families made up by roommates, an overall feeling of isolation and loneliness, resentment toward God and men for their single state, and so on. There is the fear that if they marry too late, they may not be able to have children or will have increased their chances of breast cancer if they become pregnant for the first time past the age of thirty. (In actuality, the odds of pregnancy decline in the late twenties.) If they do become pregnant at a later age, the baby's chances of Down's syndrome increase, as well as other complications down the road.

Those of us who prefer the truth, the whole truth, and nothing but the truth in order to be set free from the harsh reality of protracted singleness are often seen as troublemakers, disturbers of the peace. When I started vocalizing some of my researched conclusions about protracted singleness to many of the single women around me, one recently married young woman told me that I just wanted to "divide" Christians. Not only was she unaware of the cost for women who remain single indefinitely, she wanted a kind of "unity" based on false niceties.

I strongly believe that those who defend the status quo over what the Bible teaches regarding marriage would do better to examine their own lukewarmness toward the truth rather than worrying about the bitterness or sorrow found in the hearts of those of us who balk at protracted singleness. Jesus had far less tolerance for neutrality and a lukewarm attitude toward truth than for genuine heavyhearted sorrow and pain.

A PREREQUISITE FOR MARRIAGE?

When contentment is touted as a viable solution for the sorrow of singleness, it doesn't take long for it to become a prerequisite for achieving marriage at all. An offshoot of this belief is what I call the doctrine of numbness. Many of us have been taught that we must become completely neutral or numb to the idea of marriage before God will bless us with it. In other words, God will not drop marriage into our laps until we are completely satisfied in him and put our desire for a spouse on the altar of sacrifice, much like Abraham offering Isaac.

The argument often goes something like this: "The Bible says that God will give you the desire of your heart. But the desire of your heart must be Jesus to be granted. If you desire marriage, it proves you don't love Jesus since the desire of your heart is misplaced."9

Did past generations that married in higher numbers at lower ages go through this kind of bargaining, jumping through hoops and over hurdles before being allowed to get married? Why does this new God of singleness desire more sacrifices on our part than the God revealed in the Bible?

The truth is that God prefers our enthusiasm and embrace of his design to lukewarm neutrality. Imagine how he feels when someone yawns and ho-hums when presented with the gospel. How would you feel if you created a wonderful gift for someone, only to have him or her regard it with cool indifference?

Why would God make us desire marriage by design and then test us to assure our ambivalence toward that very design? Adam's stunned response to Eve ("Wow!") is a model of how we should respond to the idea of marriage itself.

Unfortunately, we have accepted the blurred line between self-interest and selfishness as normal. Under the simplified platitudes of "Don't touch, don't taste, don't handle!" we readily think it has to be all Christ and never us. The moment we want something in addition to Christ, we think he's out to get us. We think that we must sacrifice everything to God, even the things he wants us to have! We forget that God is the one who instituted marriage to bless us.

Self-interest is not selfishness. Self-interest only becomes unholy when we organize our lives apart from God. Organizing our lives with the goal of achieving marriage reflects God's agenda far more accurately than having a carefree, neutral attitude toward it and refusing to pursue what he's clearly shown is his will for us. Here it comes yet again—God made us to need marriage, just as he made us to need oxygen, food, shelter, clothing, work, children, and friends. We must cooperate in pursuing his will for us.

Hannah wanted a baby. Jacob wanted a wife. They didn't apologize for pursuing their self-interest; God gave them those desires in the first place. Killing the self never requires the abandonment of self-interest, only of self-ishness. When we lump the two together, it's all too easy to label the person unhappy with singleness as ungrateful, discontented, or selfish.

A Word of Warning

We must be very careful in how we approach teaching about this issue, for God says that forbidding marriage is a doctrine of demons. Note what Paul had to say:

> Now the Spirit expressly says that in later times some will depart from the faith by devoting themselves to deceitful spirits and teachings of demons, through the insincerity of liars whose consciences are seared, who forbid marriage and require abstinence from foods that God created to be received with thanksgiving by those who believe and know the truth. For everything created by God is good, and nothing is to be rejected if it is received with thanksgiving, for it is made holy by the word of God and prayer. (1 Timothy 4:1-5, emphasis added)

I anticipate that those who defend the status quo on singleness will retort that they did not forbid marriage but only told singles to not over-elevate marriage in hopes that then they would not be overly disappointed for not being married.[10] In other words, be neutral. We cannot escape the fact that this new doctrine actually creates an artificial tension between the Maker and something that he declared to be good. They make marriage appear to be in competition with the One who made it. It is not.

Express Yourself!

I can't encourage you strongly enough to be honest about how you feel about your singleness. Don't put a good face on it and stuff your true feelings deep inside. Like David, pour out your heart to your God and be real about your needs. God desires your openness and honesty about your desire—not a false ambivalence toward a purpose he set for you, his beloved child.

CHAPTER 9

"Being Single = Knowing and Serving God Better"

*H*ave you ever had that dream in which you're running and running and never get to where you're going? When I was single, I always felt like the finish line of marriage kept being pushed back. Just as I got close enough almost to reach it, it moved a few feet ahead. Somehow it was never my turn to be married.

People at church always had an explanation. "This is a good character-building experience, Debbie," they'd say. "God must be teaching you to be patient and to wait on him." Those without a specific answer always had the same question: "What do you think God is trying to teach you in all this?" As if God were holding back a husband for me until I learned the right number of lessons!

I was repeatedly asked if it might be a good idea to abandon my successful law career and go to seminary instead. *Sure!* I'd think. *That would solve everything. What's a husband compared to an M.Div.?* Or how about working in the church nursery? Like holding someone else's baby was supposed to make me feel better about not having one of my own! It seemed unfair that I had to convince people again and again that I wasn't required to come up with more activities or schooling to keep myself busy until Mr. Right miraculously showed up on the scene.

TIME TO SPARE

I never understood why I was expected to pull such a large ministry load just because I was single. It's not like being single automatically gives you more hours in a day than a married person. Not having a family doesn't mean more time on your hands; it means that you alone bear all of the responsibility of living in today's world instead of sharing it with a spouse. A married couple can divide labor to accomplish daily tasks more efficiently. Instead of having a helper, a single person bears the sole burden of laundry, housecleaning, cooking, paying bills, grocery shopping, running errands—and working to support herself. When I was single, life was often so busy there was hardly any time left for anyone or anything else, let alone ministry.

Part of this misconception about singles being able and available to serve God better than married people comes from misunderstanding 1 Corinthians 7:32-34, where Paul asserted that remaining single leaves time for doing things for God. We fail to examine the circumstances under which Paul was writing and instead assume that being single leaves lots of empty time to be filled with service. Remember, Paul was writing his advice with the foreboding recognition of famine and imminent persecution. In circumstances like those facing the Corinthians, single people would comparatively have had a lesser load than their married counterparts.

I believe another reason that we as single people are pressured to fill our lives with ministry activities is because we—as a church—have misunderstood God and his role in marriage. Under the guise of placing the entire process of marriage squarely in God's hands, often many refuse to take action, sit back, and wait for him to act.

The logic goes something like this: God has decided who will be married, and he will grant marriage for those people in his perfect time. To keep God from appearing wasteful if the wait gets too long, we insist that the single years aren't in vain—God is working out some other part of his plan in the meantime. Instead of owning up to the misuse of free will and the collective sin that has delayed marriage for so many, we spin protracted singleness as a valuable opportunity to commit one good deed after another. Once we've met our quota we can get married. So let's get serving!

This is why so many singles are placed on the front lines of church service, and why we often serve so willingly. When we ask, "What in the world do I have to do to get married?" and are told to serve, no wonder we're the first to sign up!

BE FRUITFUL AND MULTIPLY

Imagine seeing something like this in the bulletin at church:

ARE YOU SINGLE?

God has a call for your life! People who have never heard the good news of salvation are waiting for you to come tell them about Jesus. Come join us as we increase the family of God overseas. As a single person, you don't have to be childless. You can give birth to spiritual children as you lead others to Christ.

Jesus said, *"The harvest is plentiful, but the workers are few."* Will you answer his call? *"Here I am. Send me!"*

I've found that singles receive the brunt of being challenged to become missionaries. Since most of us haven't received a true call to singleness, I doubt that we've received a blanket call to missions. God's original vision was not for us to travel to remote Africa; his original vision was for us to marry and procreate.

The assumption that a call to singleness and a call to missions go hand in hand is a common one. In Scripture, we do see that Paul and Barnabas were exempted from marriage to do the kind of full-time missionary work unsuitable for a married man. But God has not established missionary work as an exemption from marriage. (Again, consider what Jesus taught in Matthew 19 on marriage and who's exempt.) Yes, some people who have received a true call to singleness may be missionaries, but obviously not all missionaries have received a call to singleness.

God's plan for kingdom expansion has always involved marriage and family. Even the New Testament gives priority to the nuclear family when it comes to increasing the kingdom: "For the promise is for you and for your children and for all who are far off, everyone whom the Lord our God calls to himself" (Acts 2:39). The early church grew as families were saved "household by household."[1]

This expansion always starts at home and works itself outward ("in Jerusalem and in all Judea and Samaria, and to the end of the earth," Acts 1:8), not the other way around. I don't believe that God's plan is to send you to the ends of the earth and bring you back home to get married once you've earned enough points. Being single by default is no reason to become a missionary by default.

Missions are important—don't get me wrong. But missionary work and church service cannot make up for the lack of fulfilling God's design. As we discussed in the last chapter, the void we have is shaped like a husband—and no amount of missionary work, Sunday school teaching, or door-to-door evangelism is going to fill it.

We are somehow expected to yearn to be removed from friends and family, to give up our future hopes of spouses and children, to relocate to the far ends of the earth where we know neither language nor culture nor a useful, self-sufficient trade—all in order to somehow prove that we are useful to God's kingdom. It doesn't make sense, and it doesn't make up for the lack of what we both want and need—marriage.

EITHER/OR VS. BOTH/AND

We do see from Jesus in Matthew 19 that some have received a call to remain single for the sake of the gospel. But it seems to me there is hardly any present-day missions work or ministry that precludes marriage today. I know lots of missionary *families*, lots of *families* who do ministry together. Marriage and ministry are not either/or propositions; they go hand in hand, remarkably so.

Before I got married, I was involved in international student ministries at my church. About 80 percent of those who volunteered were married; only 20 percent of us were single. Even the teenaged children of some of these families helped with the ministry, baby-sitting and entertaining the children of some of the younger couples while they taught English to these students.

As I look back on that time, I realize that being single in no way better equipped me for that ministry than those who were married. In fact, God works beautifully through families who minister together.

On a short-term missions trip to the Czech Republic, I found that our host missionary family agreed. Their children are the ones bringing fruit to bear in their ministry. Their children picked up the language more quickly and adjusted to a new culture with greater ease. Their children brought native school friends home, and the parents of those friends come by to meet them when picking up their children—a wonderful opportunity to develop new friendships and minister to national families. This family has lived out Joshua's challenge: "As for me and my house, we will serve the LORD" (Joshua 24:15).

Think of Billy Graham, a married man who still managed to have a great impact on evangelism and missions. Few missions or ministry activities today require singleness. Being single doesn't allow for more ministry than being married; we cannot use ministry or missions work as a justification or excuse for remaining unmarried without a specific call to singleness.

GOD REVEALS HIMSELF THROUGH FAMILY

There's a belief out there that I call rugged individual spirituality, claiming that we know and serve God better as an individual in relationship with God—that knowing and seeking God are the only real priorities we have as believers. This idea is based on verses like Matthew 6:33 where we're told to "seek first the kingdom of God" and Philippians 3:8-9, where Paul considers everything a loss compared to knowing God.

This belief leaves the impression that knowing God can occur with or without a spouse and that efforts to get married are actually secondary—and even contradictory—to seeking and knowing God. It becomes a choice between a husband and God. The problem I find with this is that God often makes himself known through familial relationships rather than individual ones. Family relationships teach us about his character.

God uses four relationships, established in Genesis 2:24, to describe himself so that we as his people will know and glorify him better. He uses the *husband-wife* relationship as the primary model to demonstrate his relationship with his redeemed people. He is the head of the relationship, providing constant spiritual, emotional, and physical well-being. He demands an exclusive love with no divided loyalties, expressing jealous anger should others creep in. He is a living sacrifice for his bride, forgiving her sins and presenting her as "holy and without blemish" (Ephesians 5:27). In the Song of Solomon he even uses the intimacy of marriage to describe his deep, passionate love for his bride.

God also uses the *father-child* relationship to demonstrate his constant provision for us, his willingness to forgive us despite our disobedience, and his use of discipline for our instruction. He delights in giving us the desires of our hearts, doesn't withhold any good thing, and is ready to give wisdom to us when we ask for it.

Lastly, God uses the *child-parent* relationship and the *wife-husband* relationship to demonstrate to us how we are to relate to him—with obedience, respect, honor, and worship.

God never says, "I love you like your teacher, your accountant, your coach, your friend, or your next-door neighbor." God never says he loves us like someone with no blood, legal, or moral ties to us—someone here today and gone tomorrow. Instead God repeatedly draws upon concrete, familial relationships and uses them as a framework from which we can understand the permanency of his love for us (Matthew 7:9-11). He loves us as his own dear children, as a husband loves his wife.

As we accept the ways in which our culture has cheapened those relationships, our understanding of God and his love for us can only diminish. What good is the love of a parent who gives up children for her own convenience or a husband who leaves on a whim?

God has purposely made himself known through familial relationships. Such relationships—husband, wife, daughter, son—show us part of the divine nature of God. When we fail to marry, whether through our own fault or cultural fault, we miss out on this means that God has established to know him more deeply and intimately.

Making a case for protracted singleness as an opportunity to know and serve God better is tantamount to the created telling the Creator that we do not care for his blueprint and that we will seek knowledge of him through any means we think correct. It divorces knowledge from obedience and goes against a primary way God has established for acquiring a more complete knowledge of him.

A Word of Encouragement

You don't have to knock yourself out in the hopes that God will reward you with a husband. You do not need to *do* anything to convince God to let you get married. God isn't sitting up in heaven dangling Mr. Right above your head, waiting for you to know him better, serve him better, become more content in him, or pack your bags for the mission field.

God has designed us to be fruitful and to multiply as we marry and begin families. As families, we can serve God just as well—if not better—than we can alone. For through marriage and family we gain firsthand knowledge and insight into God and his love for us.

CHAPTER 10

"Single = Celibate"

Let me be totally honest with you. Though I got married at age thirty-one, I really could have used a husband at sixteen, seventeen, nineteen, twenty-one, twenty-three, twenty-five, twenty-seven, twenty-nine, thirty. Especially at twenty-five—a year of numerous cold showers. Let's be honest, being single doesn't make you not want sex. Whoever said that age thirty-four is a woman's sexual peak needs to be shot.

Take a look at what singles around the country have said about sex:

> Telling a single person to celebrate their singleness as a gift from God, to wait, that God will fulfill the desires of their heart when the years and the biological clock prove otherwise, and ignoring the very basic and God-given sexual drives inherent in every human is naive and unfair and is yet one more reason why the church . . . is not salt or relevant in the world. . . . When the years pass with no spouse and no children . . . the truth is exposed, it is disillusioning.

> We Protestants might as well set up monasteries and nunneries of our own, rather than (in some cases) have duplicitous lives filled with fornication, or (in other cases) lives of obedient chastity, yet filled with an adjoining quiet desperation and depression.

Despite how singles like these are feeling, whenever teachers address sexual frustration, the advice turns to avoidance—turn off the television, put down the romance novel, drive the long way home to avoid that billboard, turn off the computer. All seemingly good ideas with one major flaw—they ignore the fact that we are hardwired by our Creator to want sex and to pursue sexual fulfillment.

I can hear the "But . . . !" on the tip of your tongue. Hang on a second, and let's go back to Genesis and what we've already established: God designed us for marriage; he designed us to want sex and to pursue sexual fulfillment *through marriage*. Sexual desire should push us toward pursuing marriage in order for that desire to be fulfilled.

Preaching abstinence to teenagers is one thing—I'm all for it as long as the message is to wait (not indefinitely) for marriage where sexual expression has full rein with God's blessing and approval. But to preach abstinence to those in protracted singleness, though technically correct, is not sound advice.

Hear me out. Celibacy and abstinence are not the same. Celibacy and singleness are not the same. Celibacy and self-control are not the same. Celibacy is a gift of God in which he has removed the drive to pursue sex.

The view that singleness and celibacy are the same thing is widespread. Many ministers seem oblivious. One offered this teaching: "If [you] have contentment through faith in God's promises . . . [p]erhaps you shouldn't seek [sexual gratification]. God may want you single."[1] According to this reasoning, if singles want sexual satisfaction through marriage, that shows they are discontented with God's promises.

It is irresponsible to preach celibacy to a group of people when very few of them have that gift *without preaching the pursuit of marriage in the same breath*. The truth is that our sexual drive was created by God and was designed to find release within marriage.

The apostle Paul understood this. He began 1 Corinthians 7 with a keen understanding of human nature and our inborn sexual drive. He taught that "each man should have his own wife" because marriage is better than "sexual immorality" (1 Corinthians 7:1-2). He acknowledged that without marriage, fornication is often the result for all of us who lack the gift of celibacy.

"Wait just a minute," you say. "I'm not a fornicator!"

Remember Jesus and the Pharisees? He said, "But I say to you that everyone who looks at a woman with lustful intent has already committed adultery with her in his heart" (Matthew 5:28). Switch this to "man" and I certainly fell into that camp. How about you?

SEX ED 101

The raging debate among educators in our current school system is whether to teach abstinence or safe sex. Both positions openly acknowledge the flaws on the other side. The safe sex crowd argues that teenagers will do it anyway, so let's assume the worst and do our best to minimize health risks. The abstinence crowd argues that premarital sex is unhealthy and immoral and that we should encourage kids to live by a higher standard of self-control.

Though this sounds self-contradictory, *both positions are right and both positions are wrong.* Those who preach safe sex are correct that human sexuality will run its natural course toward expression; they are wrong to conclude that sex should be condoned and subsidized outside of marriage. Those who preach abstinence are correct that sex outside of marriage is destructive; they are wrong to believe that we can convince kids to delay sexual fulfillment indefinitely. Both positions have proved the other's failure.

I personally agree with the position of abstinence. But we need to acknowledge that it's not working as well as we'd like. We can't see its failures as simply a lack of dedication or commitment on the part of teenagers; they are smack-dab in the middle of a culture—and often families—where commitment doesn't hold much value. How can we expect kids to honor commitment when their own parents are modeling the exact opposite?

I think there are two primary reasons why abstinence is not working. First, the vow of abstinence is on a collision course with teens' very nature; and, second, they have no hope.

There was a time when people married and started families in their late teens and early twenties. That sounds awfully young to us today, but there was a time when children were raised so that their emotional and physical development coincided. As their sexuality began to develop, marriage was just around the corner. But in today's culture of protracted adolescence, children are raised to remain adolescent, stay in school indefinitely, and live at home as "adult children," delaying marriage and adulthood. Despite all this, they are fully grown with fully adult desires. Because their very natures will drive them to seek adult pleasures, the only way to subdue and delay sexual gratification is if the hope of marriage actually exists. The concept of deferred gratification only works so long as there is the future prospect of gratification. What's the point of waiting for something that may never come?

We are lying to adolescents if we tell them to save themselves for marriage when at the same time we are telling their older siblings stuck in protracted singleness that singleness and celibacy are the same thing. Any fifteen-year-old looking at the average twenty-five-year-old single will hardly be inspired to wait for marriage. The sheer hopelessness of seeing that marriage isn't going to come any time soon becomes incentive to pursue immediate gratification. I'll say it again: Why wait for something that may never come?

THE WAY IT IS

I know some Christian women in their late twenties who are resentful of the fact that they maintained sexual purity. Go ahead, read the previous sentence again. Yep, they are sorry they stayed sexually pure. Intellectually they know they've obeyed God's commands about saving sex for marriage, and of course they did the right thing, but they're still mad about it. Their anger is just below the surface—they're not sure they want to reward a future spouse with their virginity. I can understand where they're coming from. Why reward a man (who is more than likely without excuse for waiting so long to marry) with virginity?

It's interesting to me that it's not only those who engage in premarital sex who end up with regrets. Without condoning their position, I can understand their frustration. And I'm acknowledging something that exists, even if we'd rather not face it.

When Lauren Winner wrote about "evangelical whores"[2] in the church, you'd have thought she was completely mad. How dare a "good Christian" advocate premarital sex? But she did no such thing!

Her article was a statement of fact about what is. She was being honest about the situation that exists in evangelical singles circles in today's churches. More than two-thirds of men and women are no longer virgins when they get married.[3] In a survey of 1,500 single Christians, only 39 percent of the women surveyed were virgins.[4] In another survey of Presbyterian and Baptist singles, only one-third had abstained from sex.[5]

Listen to what one single confessed:

> What do we do as supposed leaders [of] Christian singles? . . . I must confess, I am two months out of an engagement that my fiancée broke off. When I confessed having sex with her to my accountability group, none were harsh with me, and all gave me ample amounts of grace. I don't know how my pastors would deal with me if they knew, and I have been told not to confess by friends. I hate being single and leading a group of singles with 20 women in it.

At the outset of 1 Corinthians 7, Paul admitted that the celibate person could be single, but that the single person probably wouldn't be celibate. He was right then, and he's right today. And yet we keep preaching sexual purity and abstinence instead of marriage. We have the solution to the problem but refuse to acknowledge it.

We often don't like this kind of honesty. These statistics expose the flaws in our understanding of human sexuality, and they highlight our unbelief that Scripture has provided a remedy for this temptation—marriage.

Bobby Bowden, a Florida football coach, is one of the few who has stood up to this truth. While being interviewed about his life, he talked about getting married at an early age by today's standards. When asked why he and his wife married so young, he freely admitted that they wanted to have sex, so they got married.[6] I love that kind of honesty!

Tell that story to most people, and you'll probably get a two-page lecture about divorce, followed by another one on contentment in singleness. But I am not talking about entering marriage lightly or blindly. I am talking about the fact that we must acknowledge human nature and have the faith to believe that God will bless those who pursue his chosen outlet for the expression of that nature.

It only takes a quick look back in history to see that the pre-Reformation Catholic Church's insistence on celibacy for the clergy didn't negate human nature. It's telling that the men and women who went to such great lengths to isolate themselves in cloistered service to God were such failures at maintaining sexual purity. It was this "sexual incontinence"[7] plaguing the clergy that the Reformers were, in part, reforming against. They believed that the Catholic Church's preference for celibacy would have serious consequences, especially for the undiscerning.[8]

Even today celibacy in the Catholic Church is fraught with problems, as recent events have proved. The entire concept of celibacy is flawed when it is demanded of people instead of affirmed in those whom God has actually equipped by removing their natural desire.

Despite these examples of failure by godly men and women who attempted to hazard singleness without the gift of celibacy, we still whitewash singles in the church today as monks and nuns capable of serving God for years and decades and staying sexually pure in the process—without ever asking if any of them received such a calling to celibacy. We cannot blind ourselves to the reality of the situation. We cannot think that serving breakfast at the soup kitchen on Saturday morning automatically means behaving like a saint on Saturday night. The solution for single adults is the same for teenagers: We must preach abstinence, but hand in hand with God's design for us to be married. There must be hope of a timely marriage for abstinence to be successful.

"LET'S JUST BE FRIENDS"

We're no longer taught that God made us "male and female," but that we are designed to be "relational."[9] As a result of thinking that we are just "individuals" designed to be "relational," we pretend that if we just relate to one another in "healthy, sexual ways" we have mastered the problem. But there is no "healthy, sexual way" to relate to one another other than having sex within marriage (which is exactly what God designed)! We cannot be satisfied with a "healthy, sexual" relationship or a "healthy, non-erotic relationship"[10] outside of marriage, because there's no such thing apart from marriage. Our church circle just cannot do for us what marriage can.

We are far removed from what Christians have historically believed. While many people today believe that Christian singles can have "healthy, non-erotic, intimate relationships" with other singles, Christians of the past would have considered the idea pure fantasy. While we today readily endorse the idea of "renewed virginity" (a period of abstinence following sexual activity), Christians in the past would have cited our desires as evidence of why God created marriage in the first place. While we often ignore the sexuality of young people and avoid teaching the remedy of marriage, Christians of the past would have argued for the mandate of marriage. It's easier to pretend that these "healthy, sexual" ways do exist than to come right out and tell someone, "Get married!"

I think it's interesting that the social sciences have dropped the "m" word, and have replaced it with "relationships," "significant others," "life partner," and so on. Our purpose is not to be "relational." Man was designed to be a husband, woman to be a wife—and that was to be their "principal" occupation.[11]

All relationships are not equal; any old relationship will *not* suffice when it comes to fulfilling the marriage mandate. To think otherwise implies that God's "male and female" ordering can be satisfied so long as we're not alone but have many relationships in many forms. Frankly, many homosexuals believe in that understanding of "relationships."

God did not design us to be third wheels to married couples or buddies for other singles. God did not create Eve to help Adam with his work and to be his friend on the evenings and weekends. She was capable of those things, but they wouldn't fulfill her purpose. Eve was designed to help Adam in his work, to remove his loneliness, to have sex with him, to create children with him—she was designed to fill Adam's wife-shaped void.

Even men who have been dead for five hundred years understood the greater value of a spouse in comparison to a friend. The philosopher Erasmus wrote that the only thing that links us to friends is the "benevolence of mind," but that with a wife "we are joined by the greatest affection, physical union, the bond of the sacrament, and the common sharing of all fortunes."[12]

I know the following is a long quote, but read how he went on to describe the benefits of marriage:

> The affection of a wife is not spoilt by faithlessness, is veiled by no pretense, is shattered by no change of fortune; in the end it is severed by

death alone, or rather not even by death. She disregards her duties to her parents and sisters and brothers out of love for you, she looks up to you alone, she depends on you, with you she would fain die. If you have wealth, you have someone to look after it and increase it; if you have none, you have someone who can seek it for you. In times of prosperity, happiness is doubled; in adversity there will be someone to console and assist you, to show her devotion, to wish your misfortune hers. Do you think there is any pleasure to be compared with so close a union? If you are at home, she is there to dispel the tedium of solitude; if abroad, she can speed you on your way with a kiss, miss you when you are away, receive you gladly on your return. She is the sweetest companion of your youth, the welcome comfort of your old age. By nature any association is pleasant for man, seeing that nature begot him for kindness and friendship. Then how can this fail to be the most pleasant of all, in which there is nothing that is not shared?[13]

Can friendship do all that? No way.

BACK TO THE BIBLE

We must start thinking critically—biblically—and realize that by encouraging people to overlook the true costs of protracted singleness, the church is selling the world's view of family, not God's. The church should not endorse the same theories as the world—that family relationships are disposable and that "family" can be reconstructed in any mold as long as consent and love are present. We cannot continue to accept the teaching that friends and church community can somehow replace the normal family structure enjoyed by past generations.

I pray you're beginning to see that much of the contemporary church is walking, talking, and thinking like the world in terms of how it views and treats singleness. We must return to a biblical model of marriage and singleness in order to offer hope to a world plagued by protracted singleness, living without hope.

If we return to biblical thinking about human sexuality, we are forced to look boldly at Jesus' open endorsement that our sexual drive is sufficient cause to marry. Our very design, including our sexual desire, is a perfectly valid and natural reason to marry.

"But," the argument goes, "a marriage based solely upon two people wanting sex is doomed to failure!" There is some merit to the argument. However, I seriously doubt that there's a burgeoning phenomenon of such marriages occurring at large today. There are much easier—and cheaper—ways to get sex these days. Even Christian believers fall into this trap.

I've seen this backward thinking in singles ministry: People commit sexual sin, deciding that it's simply easier to meet a need now and ask for forgiveness later than to deal with the hassle of getting into a marriage that will probably end in divorce. This is exactly the kind of thinking and behavior that Matthew 19 forbids. Paul also condemned such backward logic: "It is better to marry than to be aflame with passion" (1 Corinthians 7:9). In that light, Jesus was not saying that sexual desire itself is the sole basis for marriage, but that such desire is part of our God-given design to drive us toward marriage. We would do well to take this seriously and to realize that instead of accepting the seemingly inevitable abysmal virginity rate, we should get a move on toward pursuing marriage.

The Bottom Line

The bottom line is that in spite of the myriad of sermons preached to single people about staying pure and saving sex for marriage, the vast majority of them overlook the limits of human endurance in either a prolonged dating relationship or in protracted singleness in general. Abstinence is great in theory, looks good on paper, and is something to which virtually every Christian can give intellectual assent. But in practical terms it is nearly impossible to achieve in this sex-crazed culture in which we live. Statistics prove this point.

Those who preach on human sexuality should not end their sermons on a note of self-control. The challenge I'm offering these leaders is to be more comprehensive in teaching by speaking frankly about the limits of our physical and sexual endurance instead of just assuming that singles are able to maintain an indefinite series of dating relationships that kindle romance while keeping their hands to themselves.

Jesus understood the limits of abstinence and encouraged marriage. Why can't today's church do the same? Martin Luther observed that if someone doesn't fall into one of the three exemptions Jesus described, that person "should not consider anything except the estate of marriage. Otherwise it is simply impossible for you to remain righteous."[14] Whenever men (and women) try to "resist" marriage, their natural impulses will run their course "through fornication, adultery and secret sins" in the futile fight against their very nature.[15]

Luther went on to say:

> Many think they can evade marriage by having their fling for a time, and then becoming righteous. . . . If one in a thousand succeeds in this, that would be doing very well. He who intends to lead a chaste life had better begin early, and attain it not with but without fornication, either by the grace of God or through marriage. . . .
>
> Why should one not forestall immorality by means of marriage? *For if special grace does not exempt a person, his nature must and will compel him to produce seed and multiply.* If this does not occur in marriage, how else can it occur except in fornication and secret sins?
>
> But, they say, suppose I am neither married nor immoral, and force myself to remain continent? *Do you not hear that restraint is impossible without special grace?* For God's word does not admit of restraint; neither does it lie when it says, "Be fruitful and multiply." . . . You can neither escape nor restrain yourself from being fruitful and multiplying; it is God's ordinance and takes its course. . . .
>
> [W]hoever finds himself unsuited to the celibate life should see to it right away that he has something to do and to work at it; then let him strike out in God's name and get married.[16]

CHAPTER 11

A Few More "Easy" Answers

Unfortunately, it seems like the "easy" answers offered to us as singles don't ever end. Each one has many variations—to fit any situation of singleness we may find ourselves in. So here are a few more answers and a look at how to respond.

"You have to be the right person to meet the right person."

This is a variation on the "Jesus is all you need," "You must be content in God alone" message. It sounds good and wise, but it presumes that God withholds a spouse for someone based on spiritual "rightness," painting an inaccurate picture of God and his plans for his people. It also represents the works-righteousness version of achieving marriage, like it's some sort of bonus incentive program for the super-sanctified. It *is* God's will that we be sanctified, but that is not a yardstick by which he measures our marriage readiness.

I can't imagine God sitting in heaven thinking, *I really wanted Jane to learn that one extra lesson in sanctification; since she failed, I guess I'll have to pass on that heart surgeon I had in mind for her.* God is our heavenly Father who loves to give good gifts to his children. Marriage is not a carrot he's holding out in hopes we'll go the extra mile.

There is danger in this answer too, because it has the potential to undermine marriages that do occur. If disappointment pops up in a marriage, it becomes all too easy to assume that it's the result of marrying the "wrong person." No-fault divorce and this false belief blend together creating a recipe for disaster.

Making contentment a prerequisite for marriage is a hypothesis that can never be proved correct. Let's say that someone finally becomes so neutral about marriage that she could say that all she wants in life is to know God better. If after a year or so she is suddenly reminded of her lack of a spouse, she fails the test. Don't pass go; don't collect two hundred dollars. If she were really content in God alone, the thought would not have occurred, the argument goes.

The only proof we have of this idea working is those who want the world to know their contentment and have convinced themselves that their righteousness has earned them Mr. Right. But we must never forget that the only righteousness we have is in Christ.

"It's better to be single than to wish you were" (and its variation, *"Marriage is hard"*).

Usually when someone told me either of these things when I was single, I just shook my head. It never made sense to me. *Why long for singleness once you're married? If singleness was so great, why did you get married in the first place?* I'd wonder. And "marriage is hard"? What made this person assume she could handle its pressures but I couldn't? Life *is* hard. So is work, so is having a baby, so is parenting, so is being alone. There are trade-offs in every station of life—challenges and benefits. No one should be discouraged from marriage or encouraged to put it on hold indefinitely just because it's hard! Most things worth having require hard work.

We cannot point to the high divorce rate and say that it's better not to marry. That's like saying you shouldn't go to high school because the dropout rate is increasing. The failure of other people's marriages is no reason to scrap marriage altogether.

We must hold our Bible teachers accountable to stop using a double standard. It's unfair to read the Song of Solomon and extol singles "not [to] stir up or awaken love until it pleases" (Song of Songs 2:7) and then ignore the rest of the song that praises the sheer, undeniable joy of romantic married life and sex. Instead of pointing to couples that found misery in marriage, teachers need to point to those Christians who have found marriage to be comfort and joy, examples that encourage marriage.

We cannot pretend that a good marriage is a random, luck-of-the-draw event, and so it's better to avoid marriage as a solution. Jesus didn't let the disciples off so easily, and we cannot escape down that route either.

"As soon as you stop looking, you'll find the right person."

This variation on the contentment idea rewrites Proverbs 18:22 to say, "He who *stumbles upon* a wife . . . obtains favor from the LORD." That's not what my Bible says. It says, "He who *finds* a wife . . . obtains favor from the LORD." Finding involves looking for something in particular, searching with a specific goal in mind, and doing so within reasonable time limitations. The truth is that most of us are always looking—consciously or not—until we find a spouse. While some confidently believe that God is *the* factor in causing marriage to occur, it does not mean that God is the *only* factor. We must search.

There's an underlying barb to this saying that anyone who is unhappily single must have been on a rampage or hunt until this point. If you're single with no prospect in sight, *you have cause for concern.* Voicing that concern in no way reflects on you as a person or implies that you're doing something wrong or that God must want you to stop so he can show you he is God. Scripture clearly demonstrates that God loves to bless godly spouse hunts. (See, for example, the story of Abraham, Isaac, and Rebekah in Genesis 24, discussed further in Chapter 13 of this book.) He is not waiting for you to end your search but instead uses your looking to get you a mate—just as he uses your hunger to get you to eat and your thirst to get you to drink.

Out of this idea comes the saying that goes like this: "Let God introduce you to your mate; let him find you a husband." Unfortunately, people don't generally walk into our lives with stickers on their shirts saying, "Hello. My name is _____. I'm the one God wants you to marry." God is not aligning the planets and getting the fireworks ready for when you meet your destiny. That's not how God works; that's reckless romanticism and an abundance of cheap romance novels at work.

The truth is that we're always being introduced to new people—from the dentist to the UPS man. In a sense, every meeting we have is a divine appointment. God gave us intelligence; it's up to us to exercise judgment and determine the reason behind each new introduction. Our free will is not in competition with God's sovereignty.

"You'll get married in God's perfect time, so just relax!"

Here's that "wait on the Lord" idea again. So if God knows the future, why pray? Since God knows where I'll work, why look for a job?

We must stop thinking that because God knows the end result, we can rely on him to work out everything in between. Of course he is able to do that. But we were not created to just sit back and retire from life as he works out the details. There is nothing wrong with finding comfort in the knowledge that God is sovereign and sitting on his throne, at work in our lives. But we cannot use good theology as an excuse to get out of the responsibilities we must take to secure our own futures—whether it means finding a job, a house, or a husband.

"My sister got married the other day, and she's thirty-seven."

During my single years this kind of story was supposed to make me feel better as I watched other friends marry and leave me still stuck in singleness. Yeah, right.

Yes, marriages do often happen later in life, but it's hard to know why Laura didn't marry sooner. Will she now have trouble conceiving and having children? Though meant as an encouragement, things like this create the impression that there's nothing wrong with marrying so late in life. It doesn't address the fact that Laura's been cheated of a husband for the last fifteen years of her life.

I'd usually offer congratulations but quietly think to myself, *I'm glad it worked out for her, but it's not ideal, and I certainly don't want to wait that long!*

I can't help but think that this idea is much like the glee you feel when you get a big tax refund. If you can forget that the government has been spending your money for the past year and that you could have been making that money work for you, you can actually view the government as a kind benefactor. But just as a tax refund is usually skimpy for most taxpayers, few of the Lauras out there will receive enough to compensate them adequately for their years of waiting.

It's true that some couples have married later in life, and we can see that God had a real purpose behind prolonging their single years. But that's the exception rather than the rule and shouldn't serve as an excuse or justification to delay marriage.

"It's God's will that you are single right now."

In order to comfort (and often condone) those who find themselves in protracted singleness, church leaders will often say something to the effect that God has ordained them to be single at this point in their lives—maybe they'll marry later and maybe they won't.

Telling an entire group of singles that God has mandated or decreed their singleness at that point in time can have the dangerous effect of justifying bad behavior. This goes back to misunderstanding God's will and sovereignty and the need to think biblically rather than culturally.

Depending on the mind-set of an individual within the audience (either pro-marriage or procrastinator), he will either entertain a shaky confidence in the will of God or a perverse pleasure in beating the marriage rap for another day.

I've said it over and over: Protracted singleness rarely glorifies God and cannot save you, sanctify you, or justify you in God's eyes.

To teach a crowd of singles that God has decreed that every single person present should be single at that moment just doesn't work because some are single because they have neglected their God-given duty to marry. Many women in the singles population today do not have any business being single—today, for the next ten years, or for the rest of their lifetimes. Without a calling from God to be single in order to accomplish a specific task for him, we have no cause to be single.

The church must stop catering to those who are single by their own desire or by default. It must stop condoning this kind of protracted singleness if it wants to have a healthy next generation of people to continue the growth of God's family and to be part of his everlasting covenant.

"There's no shame in being single."

While this may be true today, it wasn't always the case. People looked askance at those who put off marriage for no apparent reason and remained single beyond the typical marriageable age. This shame or stigma placed on singles (particularly on men) had the benefit of encouraging or prompting people to begin their adult lives by marrying and starting families.

If one thinks about it, this kind of a statement is really a sort of cheap flattery today, a flattery that does not solve the problems associated with protracted singleness. Instead of looking for ways to endorse an otherwise abnormal state, singles should be told how to stop this cycle.

"Dating is fun!"

Not hardly!

Dating may have been fun in high school and early college. But once you start hitting your mid- to late twenties, dating loses its luster. As Carrie mused on *Sex and the City*, "When did dating go from being fun to being scary?"

If dating is so much fun, why do so few singles actually date (one on one, not in groups), especially as the years go on? The truth is that dating is not only not fun, it's unfair to women. (We'll say more about that in the next chapter.)

GETTING SERIOUS ABOUT GETTING MARRIED

Changing the way we think about singleness and marriage is essential to ending the love affair we've accepted with protracted singleness. Examining Scripture to see what God has intended for marriage and applying its truth to our lives is vitally important.

In the next section of the book, we'll look at ways we can begin to order our lives around the biblical principles we've discovered. How will our thinking affect our behavior as we put into practice the things we have learned? How can we live in a way that reflects our pursuit of marriage?

PART 3

Getting Serious

A B O U T

Getting Married

CHAPTER 12

Saying No to the Dating Game

*I*magine that you're an employer looking to hire someone to be the president of your company. Resumés come in, and you find one that looks promising. You decide he may be perfect for the job—his current employment, age, looks, and past experience seem promising—with one problem. You have no way to verify his work experience. Was he a great worker, someone to be trusted? Or was he lazy, sloppy, and fired by each one of his previous employers?

With no way to check out his credentials, your only option is to spend the next six months interviewing this one candidate before you feel comfortable enough to offer him the position. If after those six months you decide he's not the right candidate for the job, you have to begin the entire process again.

How frustrated would you be if you had to go through that multiple times? Yeah, that's what I thought.

There is no consensus in the Christian world on dating—at what age it's appropriate to start (if ever), the true purpose behind it (from fun and recreation to searching for a spouse), the norms and codes of its practice (for example, who calls to ask for a date). Despite all the differing opinions about it, dating in all its various forms represents the present system we have to find a spouse. I think it's a broken system, and it's time to call it quits.

Despite the fact that men often resent dating because they have to foot the bill, I believe women pay a much higher price. As a means to securing a spouse, dating is unfair to women because it often does not

145

accomplish its goal of marriage and leaves women vulnerable to remaining indefinitely single.

Dating Is Inefficient and Not Very Effective

It seems to be a given among most people today that it takes an unlimited—and possibly an untold—number of dates before it's time to head for the altar. It can take years and even decades before dating ends and marriage begins. All this dating has left women tired. As Charlotte said on *Sex and the City*, "I have been dating since I was fifteen. I am exhausted. Where is he?" When is it time to quit dating and get married? Without an answer, the indefinite waiting leads to frustration.

Whether we lead the wild lives portrayed on *Sex and the City* or lead lives of quiet desperation, we are tolerating a high level of inefficiency. I would go so far as to say that we even tolerate a high level of incompetence and the absence of desired results; we embrace a system that we openly acknowledge has no guarantees of producing a husband at all. Because it is firmly believed that you *have* to go through a series of dating relationships before settling down to marriage, we do.

Why do we tolerate it? I can't think of any other system in our lives that we allow to be so dysfunctional. We'd certainly never go through the hassle of house hunting without first being hopeful that we could find something within our price range. We'd not go through the time and expense of college without knowing we'd earn a degree when we completed the program.

Some people argue that there is a benefit to this inefficiency. By staying single longer, some believe the quality of an eventual marriage will be better or the chances of divorce lower. However, experts suggest that while it is best to wait until the early twenties to marry, no additional benefits are found from further delaying marriage to the late twenties or thirties. The "data fail to prove any benefit increasing the age of marriage beyond 22."[1] Some also believe that by staying single longer, there is more peace in the ultimate decision of whom to marry. We either claim to have met the right one or we claim that, having considered all the possibilities, we made the best and most informed choice. Of course, the downside to all this is that after years of serial dating, we can go on to repeat the cycle with no guarantee that we'll meet Mr. Right in the next year, or two, or ten.

Because dating is the primary method for finding a husband, we have an inherent need to rationalize its lack of efficiency. We ask ourselves questions like, "What did I learn from that relationship?" "What about him do I want in a husband?" "What about him *don't* I want in a husband?" We push to stay friends after a dating relationship ends so that the time we've spent wasn't a total waste.

We assume that a lesson learned—no matter how small—offsets the time and personal investment lost in the process. We grasp for some benefit, even as we know that nothing more can be gained from continued association with a guy who clearly turned out to be "Mr. Wrong."

Because people date for many different reasons—for fun with no strings attached, for sexual experimentation within a meaningful relationship, for someone to take care of you because your mom won't anymore, or for finding a spouse—it's hard for a woman to find out if the man she's dating has the same motivation.

Of course, even if they are on the same page, it takes time to discover all those hidden traits that aren't so apparent at first. Is he a slob? Cheap? A pervert? A drunk? Granted, he may not be any of those things and be nearly perfect. But if he's not, many women throw good time after bad, hoping to change or reform him without success. And then it's time to send him packing and start the cycle again, this time hoping the flaws won't be so major.

Dating Promotes a Lack of Equality

In its most prevalent form, dating is initiated by men who pursue women for companionship, sex, living together, or marriage. Though many people believe that it's perfectly okay for women to initiate a dating relationship, the simple fact is that most women don't.

Because that's the way it is, a man has the ultimate balance of power in dating. He looks around at his leisure, decides who he thinks is the most physically and emotionally attractive, and asks her out for a date— all on his timetable. A woman waits for a man to become interested, and when and if he asks her out, her only power is a decisional one—whether or not to accept his invitation.

There are no real checks and balances. A woman feels pressured into accepting invitations from less than worthy candidates. Her veto power isn't much of a bargaining chip, because the downside of saying no is losing more time until the next offer comes in.

Sally was in her late thirties, owned her own home, and had a respectable job and a decent savings account. She was dating someone who, though older, was a pizza delivery boy. I was shocked. She actually became engaged to this individual, which was even more shocking. At some point she looked up and thought, *This isn't fair.* The engagement ended, and I have to admit I was relieved.

Women are generally beholden to men for asking them out, and men are indirectly encouraged to seek out women slightly above them. Who's going to stop them? Since prospective suitors know they will not meet a woman's family on the front end, they can take the gamble of aiming high and hope to get lucky. In the past men would not have been so bold because a girl's parents would tell any suitor beneath her to scram.

Dating doesn't put men and women on a level playing field. Women cannot control which man is interested, when he gets interested, or the direction of the relationship without issuing ultimatums—"Let's get married or break up." And then she's back where she started—waiting for someone to be interested. Not a good place to be.

DATING LEADS TO UNRECOVERABLE LOSSES

When dating continues like this, something is often lost that can rarely be recovered. I'm not just referring to virginity, which is lost by many women before marriage. I'm talking about time, trust, innocence, and passion. As the differences between the sexes become blurred, women sometimes deaden their senses to maintain dating's reputation as merely "casual."

Dating *might* lead to something more—marriage—but it doesn't have to. In the meantime we're told to just hang in there and that it will all work out in the end. Women are forced to become more and more detached in order to survive—keeping their emotions in check, lowering their expectations, caring some but not too much. Eventually those emotional characteristics that set us apart as women begin to disappear.[2]

Women showing up at the altar today have often previously experienced a number of mini-divorces as a result of dating, even if there's no paperwork to prove it. As Barbara Dafoe Whitehead has said, the "emotional residue" of chronic breakups is painfully obvious.[3] We cannot continue to believe that setting boundaries is enough to offset the costs of dating. Though a good word of caution, telling women not to put too much of an "emotional investment"[4] into dating denies our female nature. We're back once more to the fact that God designed us for marriage. It's our nature to want it. And because that's how God made us, that's what we're invariably looking for as we date.

Believing that we are able to successfully guard our hearts from hurt through a maze of dating relationships is like believing that seat belts save lives in airplane crashes. Telling women to go through relationship after relationship, all the while suppressing their hopes and natural affection, is akin to telling someone to eat without taste buds.

If this were actually possible, we'd all be friends with our ex-boyfriends rather than decorating their photographs with horns and fangs. Just the fact that we need time to recover and heal after a breakup shows that something was lost in the process.[5] Rarely do we look back on past relationships and think, *I'm really glad I got to know that guy; my life is so much better because of dating him.* Instead we wish we hadn't wasted our time and that someone had warned us ahead of time.

DATING CAUSES FATIGUE

Dating isn't fun. Sure, it *was* fun in high school. But the longer you date, the less fun it is.

When I was single and bemoaning the whole idea of dating, my friends who had married in their early twenties couldn't understand. They'd go on and on about how much *fun* they'd had dating in high school and in college. How much *fun* they'd had dating their future husbands. And for *fun*, I just wanted to deck them!

I don't think they understood that it was by the sheer grace of God in such a bankrupt system that they were spared. When you marry at an early age, the memories of the past are fewer and quickly absorbed and forgotten in the midst of enjoying your husband. Having forgotten what's-his-name, it's easier to remember fondly all the relationships preceding an early marriage.

On the other hand, the longer you wait to get married (by choice or by default), the more costs there are to absorb, and their compounding nature often becomes too heavy and painful to take. Past a certain point I don't think single women can ever put on rose-colored glasses when looking at the past. Those casual exchanges once labeled *fun* become historical landmarks pointing back to a youth gone by with nothing—and no one—to show for it.

My friend Aimee has longed for a husband since college. Now in her early thirties, she dreads going on dates and wonders if her time is better spent in front of the television or playing with her dog.

This is protracted singleness, warts and all. It leads to what Whitehead calls "relationship fatigue . . . a weariness" that often cannot summon the strength to go on another date.[6] (No wonder men complain of women often being clinical and perfunctory in their relationships and begin searching for the issue-less Russian bride.)

In the past there was some method to the madness of who stayed single and became an "old maid"; looks and a fiercely independent spirit were usually the predominant traits shared by those who were unmarried. Today we have *de facto* spinsterhood, in which random women—many of whom are incredibly beautiful and not overly independent—are still single with no apparent explanation. Singleness is no longer for the ugly, the cruel, and the indifferent.

DATING DEVALUES MARRIAGE

Parents jokingly talk about having shotguns ready for the moment a boy approaches their daughter. But when we view dating as a process for finding a spouse, we must admit that teenagers have no reason to date since they are not in a position to be married. I believe that we must outline dating as a serious adult activity with a specific goal in mind—marriage.

When we are unwilling to define dating by this intended purpose, we send the message to young people that dating is casual. When we as women have been trained in this school of thought from the beginning, it is hard for us to then hold men accountable to the fact that a dating relationship *should* lead to marriage. To do so makes us look like we've turned the tables or changed the rules on them halfway through the game.

By participating in the dating system from an early age without limiting the access we give men or demanding a clear definition of dating's purpose, we can stop ourselves from getting a commitment later. If we want fun rather than a serious relationship from dating and accept that paradigm at an early age, it gets harder to switch the rules when we're ready for marriage. Having conditioned young men to plain old, no-commitment fun for years, we can't cry foul later when we find these same men are not wanting to settle down and marry according to our plans and desires. Men are left wondering why it has to be all or nothing. The reason they think this is because for the longest time dating didn't have to be anything—or even have a purpose.

I believe that such a casual attitude toward dating leads to a casual attitude toward marriage. We often give something value based upon how hard we had to work for it. To treat dating lightly reduces the value placed on marriage.

Dating Forces Women to Pretend

Dating often forces women to be disingenuous and to pretend to be disinterested in marriage. Consider what Danielle Crittenden wrote in her book *What Our Mothers Didn't Tell Us*:

> Alas, it is usually at precisely this moment—when a single woman looks up . . . and realizes she's ready to take on family life—that men make themselves most absent. . . . So long as a woman is willing to play a man's game at dating—playing the field, holding men to no expectations of permanent commitment—men would be around; they would even live with her! But the moment she began exuding that desire for something more permanent, they'd vanish. I suspect that few things are more off-putting to a man eating dinner than to notice that the woman across the table is looking at him more hungrily than at the food on her plate—and she is not hungry for his body but for his whole life.

So the single woman is reduced to performing the romantic equivalent of a dance over hot coals: She must pretend that she is totally unaware of the hot rocks beneath her feet and behave in a way that will convince a man that the only thing she really wants is the furthest thing from her mind.[7]

DATING GIVES MEN TOO MUCH TIME AND TOO LITTLE ACCOUNTABILITY

Teresa dated the same guy all the way through college. After graduation he decided to pursue a career that required more schooling and training. They'd talked of marriage and a life together, so she waited for him to propose . . . and waited. After ten years of dating each other exclusively, he said that he was sorry, but he just wasn't ready to get married.

When men say that they're "just not ready" to get married after dating one woman for a long period of time, it often goes unchallenged.

I believe that this kind of behavior is foolish. In the Bible there is no escaping that foolishness is a sin. While many people reading Proverbs assume that the fool is recklessly squandering only wealth, I believe the actions of a fool go further. Wealth can always be reacquired. But what about those who squander their youth—and someone else's youth along with their own? Lost time can never be regained.

"But I have issues I need to deal with before getting married!" a man says. In my book that's no excuse. Take care of them on your own time before you start dating and end up wasting someone else's time. But men don't feel the compulsion to give you a disclaimer up front: "Hey, I'd love to ask you out. But before you say 'yes,' I have to tell you that I get cold feet every time I hear the 'm' word. I'm just not ready for that kind of a commitment. And I have a few other issues to work out too; so you might be in for a rough ride with me. How about dinner on Friday?"

Of course, men often say they don't know what they're looking for in a wife and that dating someone for a year or two gives them a chance to figure it out. If she's not "the one" after a year or two—or ten—he backs out. In most cases, it doesn't take that long to figure it out; he's just delayed the inevitable, wasting his time and hers.

It's not that men don't ever want to get married. There are men—young men—out there who want to pursue marriage and family as quickly as possible. But so many men have set up a deadline way off in the future and have no problem dating a number of women between finishing college and reaching their marriage deadline. At that point it seems like they often marry the next woman to come along. After years of "wait and see if someone better comes along" they aren't even particularly good negotiators in securing the best possible wife.

I have a hard time believing that men today meet "the one" at twenty-nine, thirty-four, or thirty-eight when men in the past did the exact same thing in their early twenties. In the not-too-distant past shame was involved if a man went out with a woman more than three or four times without the intention of marriage. His reputation was mud, and other women would refuse him once they were made aware of his uncommitted nature. With no sense of shame (or purpose) today, men can hop, skip, and jump from one girlfriend to the next, while women are told to wait on the Lord.

It's amazing that a man can be in the dating game for three, four, five, ten, or twenty years and have absolutely nothing to show for it. If a man were to conduct his own business in the same manner, the IRS would clamp down after three years and declare the business to be just a hobby. It is precisely because most men know they can keep running a negative balance sheet—without giving any explanation—that this behavior continues. They don't have to demonstrate an active search or a good understanding of women who suit them or show that they have the end goal of marriage in mind.

When we date and settle for noncommitted, open-ended relationships not geared toward pursuing marriage, we are continuing to make dating a system doomed to failure. So what do we do instead?

JUST SAY NO

We have to stand up and say no—no to operating in the current dating system without question or constraint and no to men who aren't serious about marriage.

"But how am I supposed to get married if I'm not dating?" Dating is the way it's mostly done today—we're pretty much stuck with the system. But we can make some changes in how we approach dating and help ourselves out. The saying goes that you never know until you ask. So let's ask some questions of the guys we date.

1) *Ask his intentions and motive.*

As grown women, our dates don't often pick us up at our parents' home and face Dad asking, "What are your intentions toward my daughter?" But there's no reason the question shouldn't be asked. But we're often hesitant to ask men about their intentions up front; instead we get to a certain point in a relationship and then issue the "Let's get married or break up" ultimatum. We have to find a middle ground.

It's hard to imagine asking a man if he wants to get married when all he's proposed is dinner and a movie. But it's not too hard to steer the conversation in that direction during the meal. Questions about his plans and goals for the future shouldn't send him running for the door. Asking him if he'd like to be married and have a family someday is a natural part of that conversation. If he turns pale and gulps his drink, it's better to know he has a commitment issue after just one dinner than after dating for a year.

And chances are this guy isn't a total stranger. It can't hurt to ask men what they think about marriage and family before you begin dating. Even if he never asks you out, you've done a favor for the next girl in line.

2) *Ask about his history.*

Ask about previous relationships and why they ended. If you're buying a car, you want to know about mileage, service history, and previous accidents. This is the rest of your life we're talking about—don't require less from a date than you would of a car dealer!

Do you have friends who know him? Ask them about him, and get all the information you can. Ask your pastor, your coworkers, people you know in common.

3) *Be honest.*

Let him know where you stand. If you're in a relationship and you want to get married, talk about it. Don't pretend that you don't want to get married just to keep him interested.

4) *Set limits.*

Set time limits with the men you date, whether it's serious or not. As I've said before, you can't get your time back when a relationship fails.

One woman I know set a limit when a boyfriend told her he wasn't sure if he was ready to marry her. Together they agreed to date for three months and at the end of that time to get engaged or break up. They acknowledged that if their relationship wasn't headed toward marriage they were keeping the other person from meeting someone who could be a potential mate.

5) *Just say no.*

When you know a guy isn't your type or worth your time, just say no. When you know he has a history of noncommitment, just say no. When you know he just wants to play at the dating game, just say no. When you know the relationship isn't going anywhere, just say no more. Don't waste your time just because you don't have anything better to do or anyone better to do it with.

With the inherent drawbacks to dating, it's time to say no. We can do these kinds of things and find some success. But if we want to really say no and change the system, it's time to look at the value of enlisting agency.

CHAPTER 13

Enlisting Agency

Since dating is so problematic, what's the alternative? Because most of us have grown up with dating as the only system available, we have a hard time imagining that what's gone on in the past may have been better. It's easy to believe that marriage-making has never come with any guarantees and has always been a game of chance—romantic roulette, if you will. Because we live with an informal and casual system, it's all too easy to believe that marriages just happen, without much thoughtful planning on our part. (This goes back again to misunderstanding the will and sovereignty of God, believing that God requires our patience rather than our active pursuit of his will for marriage.)

Since we know that past generations married in greater numbers and at earlier ages, let's look at how they pursued those marriages. Would their method work for us today?

"Are you talking about arranged marriages? Are you crazy?" you ask. Stick with me here. That's not exactly what I'm proposing. *I am proposing that limited and guarded access to women produces responsible, wise, and efficient decision-making from men, while unlimited and unchecked access produces complacency and generally unwise behavior—exactly where we are today.* Anything that is too widely available is generally thought of as invaluable. Think about fashion trends. The latest thing sported by celebrities is only popular when it's hard to get. Once everyone has one, no one wants it anymore.

The Bible supports this assertion. Take the stories of Isaac and Rebekah, or Jacob and Rachel. In Isaac's story, the Bible makes it clear that in his grief over Sarah's death, Abraham had somehow neglected his duty to help Isaac find a godly wife (Genesis 24). When Abraham realized it was time to take some action, Isaac was forty years old. Abraham didn't wait on the Lord to provide a wife for his son; he didn't wonder whether it was God's will for Isaac to marry; he didn't worry that Isaac's marrying might convey that he was not fulfilled in God alone or that Abraham himself didn't trust God. No, Abraham realized that Isaac was lonely and needed a wife. So he set about planning thoughtful actions to find a wife for his son.

Abraham began to search—a deliberate, planned, purposeful search. He entrusted a servant (an agent if you will) to go back to their homeland to look for a suitable girl for his son. Though he didn't know if he would be successful, the servant carried out his objectives with thoughtful planning and prayer. He loaded up a caravan of gifts to show Isaac's financial success—something that would entice any young woman to take notice and assuage the fears of any future in-laws. The servant set himself up near a well, a highly visible and trafficked place, to increase his chances of running into prospective brides. And the servant invited the help of God Almighty, who led Rebekah to that exact spot at that exact time. We see God's sovereignty working hand in hand with human action to achieve the right result.

We know how the story ended. Abraham's agent asked permission from Rebekah's people and from Rebekah herself, both of which were given. The rest, as they say, is history. Is this an arranged marriage? Probably. God blessed their marriage, and we see that "he loved her. So Isaac was comforted after his mother's death" (Genesis 24:67).

The issue is not that they had arranged marriages and we have dating. What's worth examining is that previous cultures had systems that fostered marriages; today we have a system that dissuades marriage. In that light, here's what we can learn from this story.

1. *A single woman wasn't as vulnerable then because she operated through the agency of her parents. With their agency involved, she had superior bargaining power.* Rebekah was under the protective covering of her parents, uncle, or clan. They were the ones making sure she was entering into a safe union. Though God led Abraham's agent to Rebekah's location, Rebekah's family would not have let her stay single much

longer. They would not leave her waiting, depreciating in beauty and fertility, for marriage to "happen." Their culture would not have allowed it. They would have begun their own search for a husband for Rebekah in a timely fashion while her youth, beauty, and fertility were considered assets. This kind of acknowledgment within the community of rules of engagement forced potential suitors to act seriously, honestly, and thoughtfully. Because she had options, a young man and his family had to act both quickly and responsibly if they hoped to make her part of their family.

2. *Access to a prospective bride was limited and conditioned upon a suitor proving his worth.* Abraham's agent knew he had to prove Isaac's worthiness and success to get Rebekah's family to agree to a match. Thus the flashy caravan and costly gifts. That's why Rebekah was given some bling—a nose ring and gold bracelets—for the seemingly commonplace kindness of drawing water for the man and his camels. These gifts were designed to communicate to Rebekah and her family that it was in her best interest to become part of Isaac's family; they demonstrated to her a promising future. This communicated that her work was appreciated and rewarded. Isaac had to put his money where his mouth was to prove his worth. Obviously more is needed in a suitor than financial wealth, but the point is, the prospective husband has to be able to provide for his family.

Just one generation later it was time for Rebekah's son, Jacob, to marry. These same two principles show up again. Rebekah urged him to return to her hometown, to take action. He took a journey, waited by the well, met Rachel—and history repeated itself. So intense was their meeting that Jacob "kissed Rachel and wept aloud" (Genesis 29:11). Jacob knew he had to prove himself if he wanted Rachel for his wife; so he agreed to work for her father for seven years. It may sound extreme, but he didn't have unrestricted access to the woman he loved, and he was willing to do whatever it took to be with her. After his seven years were up, Jacob immediately asked for his wife to lie with her. There are no pretenses here. A lack of access certainly reminded Jacob of the perks of marriage.

These two stories show that past cultures understood that men and women need each other and were helpful in assisting men into marriage—either by taking action on their behalf or by encouraging them to take action themselves. These cultures also promoted marriage as families limited access to their daughters until men proved themselves worthy. This forced men to grow up, to be mature, financially stable, and responsible, and to act wisely and quickly instead of waiting indefinitely for marriage to occur.

The Bible does include stories of women who didn't have a family agency working on their side, showing the vulnerability of flying solo. The story of Ruth demonstrates what happens to women who don't have a father figure to speak on their behalf. Ruth's mother-in-law, Naomi, an elderly woman herself, hardly qualifies as an adequate covering with bargaining power because her idea of sending Ruth to the threshing room floor in the middle of the night was fraught with danger, physical harm, and costs to Ruth's reputation. There must have been a better way to remove the dibs of any other kinsman-redeemer than sneaking around in the dark, unguarded and vulnerable.

Though Naomi was shortsighted in some respects, her genuine concern for Ruth's marital state cannot be doubted. It's clear she wanted to make herself useful to Ruth in helping her find "rest . . . in the house of her husband" (Ruth 1:9). Despite Naomi's misguided plan, everything worked out for Ruth, primarily because of the integrity of Boaz and the Lord's special protection.

The story of Ruth does not prove the oft-cited moral that if one follows the God of Israel, she will be rewarded with a husband in due time. The story of Ruth points out the vulnerable situation of women who have no male authority figure to bargain for them. Ruth represents a widow in a rather exceptional situation. Rachel and Rebekah represent much more accurately what God intends for us through the protection of family and an active and negotiating father. By looking at the contrast, it's easy to conclude that it's far better to be in the protected place of Rachel and Rebekah than in the perilous position of Ruth.

Placing biblical wisdom and example aside, every culture before ours has understood that women are vulnerable in the marriage-making process. As a result, past practices shielded and protected women.

Earlier forms of courtship in this country limited a man's access to a woman based upon his demonstration of worthiness. Women were protected and could only receive a gentlemen suitor in the presence of chaperones, usually their parents. Men automatically knew that their continued association with a young woman required noble reasons and that their access would be constantly checked, rechecked, and manipulated if need be to reach the right result. These kinds of buffers kept men on the straight and narrow. It forced them to aim wisely in the women they pursued and to take the leadership and responsibility to see a relationship move toward marriage.

What I'm talking about is not that antiquated. Even as recently as the early twentieth century, this country still had a practice of courtship referred to as "calling" by sociologists. Beth Bailey, in "From the Front Porch to the Back Seat," describes "calling" as the practice of a mother issuing a "call" to a prospective gentleman to visit her daughter and their family. A budding union was always kept under the family's watchful eye. A woman's family understood that it was their duty to see her into marriage with a man worthy of her. With calling/courting, the man was the one who had to wait for a "call" and then do everything within his power to prove himself to a young woman and her family.[1]

As Danielle Crittenden says, "Almost all adults in a young woman's life conspired, whether she liked it or not, to protect her from predatory male sexual advances and romantic recklessness."[2] In this mother-controlled system, a mother took the initiative, and she could refuse a caller from returning if he had failed in what Bailey calls the subtle tests of "suitability, breeding, and background."[3] Families guarded the interests of their daughters without leaving them vulnerable or appearing cold in a rejection. In the system of courtship, it was the man who waited by the phone and did anything and everything to present himself as a good catch and a suitable spouse.

During the 1920s, dating began to replace the practice of courtship. Bailey describes this change: "Young men and women went out into the world together, enjoying a new kind of companionship and the intimacy of a new kind of freedom from adult supervision."[4] With the change from her turf to the man's turf, the distribution of power and control moved from her family to the man, who had no binding to her. As the dynamics between men and women changed to give the man more power, it is not hard to see why these courtships no longer led to marriages. Marriage is now up to the goodwill and good intentions of some random young men as opposed to being under the supervisory control of loving parents who have cared for their daughter since birth.

Hence protracted singleness. The virtually unlimited access men have into women's lives, and sometimes even into their wombs, has bred this stifling complacency.

In her book *Why There Are No Good Men Left: The Romantic Plight of the New Single Woman*, Barbara Dafoe Whitehead describes the situation for today's single women who hope to marry someday:

> Thus, when their thoughts and priorities focus on finding someone they would want to spend their life with, they don't find the kind of supporting social system for their love lives that they've enjoyed in their school and early work lives. The process of finding a life partner is often chaotic, unintelligible, and full of unexpected twists. There are no common standards or codes of behavior. There are few models or mentors. There is no operating manual that provides instruction or guidance. There is no institutional infrastructure to make it easier to realize their goals.[5]

She goes on to say that the single woman "faces a quandary: she isn't able to rely on the earlier courtship system. It no longer exists."[6] A new system has replaced the old, informing women that they must cycle through a series of "short-term, shallow," and "low commitment" relationships.[7] We no longer live in a culture that protects and promotes our desire to marry, but one that shames it, calling us "needy" or "obsessive."[8]

So, what can we do about this today? The bottom line from past cultures is that *limited access produces marriages, while unlimited access produces protracted singleness.* It pays to operate under some sort of agency—we need and should want someone else to bargain on our behalf. The other lesson to be learned from the past is that women physically lived under some sort of covering.

The Proper Covering of a Family Home

Most women today take on a lifestyle that in the past was relegated to spinsters. We live alone, are financially independent, and are in charge of our own lives. It seems to me that it then becomes somewhat predictable that we become "*de facto* spinsters." We cast off the covering of our families and engage in a period of intermediate independence, which society deems absolutely essential to both the completion of our adulthood experience and allegedly necessary to prevent any later regrets about marriage.

Whatever our motives, or whether our parents kicked us out because of the slavish American devotion to developing "independence," if we accept this pattern, we are responsible for our arrangements and must bear the consequences.

I realize the impact of what I have said here, and perhaps you're wondering whether I'm advocating that Christian single women move back in with their parents. I am definitely advocating they don't move out. But if you already live apart from your family, then, yes, I am advocating moving back in with your parents if possible. Of course, I realize the limitations of such a decision, especially since many of us don't even live in the same state as our parents, or we come from divorced families, or we already own our own homes. It's not possible for everyone.

I just don't want women who voluntarily choose to go with mainstream America on this and engage in a period of intermediate independence to then wonder what happened when they wait for marriage that fails to appear. We intentionally go in a direction that is sure to hold more negative consequences (though we don't realize it), and then we expect God's grace to make up the difference. Just like the young men of our generation making foolish decisions about marriage for a decade or more, we are banking on the Lord's comprehensiveness in providence to somehow override all of our recklessness just because he can.

The Genesis model of marriage intimates that the perfect pattern is for both the man and woman to leave their respective homes to make a new home together. They don't leave home to engage in a period of single years to sow their wild oats (in some cases), test the limits of their independence, have a career, and then at some arbitrary point in the future pair up and live happily ever after. When we unquestioningly participate in such independence, we are flirting with danger and the prospect that many of us will fall victim to permanent singleness.

I believe that the primary reason marriages do not form today is because, just as familiarity breeds contempt, access breeds complacency. Our solo living arrangements send a signal to men that they can have access into our lives and apartments at any time, and perhaps with enough time they may even be able to break down the walls of sexual abstinence. (I realize that not all men are trying to convince the woman to have sex, but sadly, many are.) The simple reason that men married in the past was not just the lack of sex outside of marriage. Sex has always been available for a price. Men married because they realized that their access to women was going to be constantly monitored by their parents.

Because access to women is virtually unlimited today, men do not see the progression of time as a threat or even a reminder to make wise decisions sooner rather than later. Men have little incentive to marry. Every function normally associated with a wife has been fragmented: food comes from take-out, sex comes from just about anywhere (for those who disregard God's moral prohibitions), and companionship comes from friends and coworkers. All this kills the sense of aloneness in young men and reduces us to a pattern of fellowshiping with one another until death do we part.

THE PROPER COVERING OF A MALE FATHER-FIGURE ADVOCATE

Rebekah and Rachel each had a father figure/agent actively working to pursue marriage on her behalf. Neither of these women was "waiting on the Lord" to work out his will or for marriage to "happen" to them. While the biblical text does not speak to any initiatives on the part of their fathers, culture simply would not allow a woman to become infertile while waiting on a young man to take some action.

This has been the way of humankind for hundreds of generations across the globe; it is only in the latter half of the twentieth century that we have abandoned this time-honored practice. In the event that neither Isaac nor Jacob had shown up, the girls' fathers would have been their scouts under their cultural norms. Even Paul acknowledged that fathers who see their daughters advancing in years and in danger of losing the full rights and benefits of marriage are required to actively seek a marital estate for their daughters (1 Corinthians 7:36, see New American

Standard Bible).[9] Similarly, even though Naomi's plan had some kinks, she repeatedly expressed legitimate concern for Ruth's future marital state. "My daughter, should I not seek rest [that is, "a home," New International Version] for you, that it may be well with you?" (Ruth 3:1).

The fact that women today operate without the protection of their parents—without their input, their support, or their advocacy—is perhaps one of the primary reasons many of us have no husbands to show for our efforts.

The main drawback to agency is that it is considered an antiquated notion, especially by today's independent woman who either accepts the assumption that her preferences would be ignored by her outdated parents or believes that she herself has the will and prowess to insure she'll get married when she wants. (Of course this begs the question, why isn't she married?)

The other disadvantage to agency is that a large portion of the church is ready to stand in the way of anyone wanting to take control of pursuing marriage. It insists that a woman must keep waiting another year, two, three, a decade for her Christian prince to emerge—otherwise, just assume the "gift" of singleness applies. Apparently for some it makes more sense to keep waiting on the fickleness of Christian men than to take wise action. It's accepted that conducting our youth with wild abandon, entrusting our outcome to men who have no binding to us, and presuming on the Lord shows more faith than employing agents or older, more fatherly Christian men to diligently search for a spouse on our behalf.

If a woman wants to be a lawyer, she can go to law school, take the Bar Exam, send out resumés to employers, and practice law. If a woman wants to run for office, she can put her name in the hat, run a good election campaign, and win the race. If a woman wants to travel to Australia, she can buy airline tickets, pack her bags, and go. In other words, she can do something to accomplish her goals. But if she wants to get married, she's told to sit like a bump on a log until the right Christian man finds her. I don't think so.

For the whole of history, marriage was under the control of the family or clan. In the past, the formation of a marriage was entrusted to the girl's guardians because they were bound and responsible before God for her welfare. By passing this duty to initiate and pursue marriage to a random young man who has no legal, ethical, or religious binding to her is like giving the city keys to a stranger.

This is the core of protracted singleness: Some men who should have been trusted the least now bear the responsibility for making marriage transpire. We must take back responsibility and encourage fathers to take the initiative to find suitable husbands for their daughters. Time is not a friend, and the rest of Scripture confirms that fullness of marriage can only be enjoyed if we marry in our youth.

Agency Worked for Me

When I realized that if I wanted my unwanted singleness to end, I was going to have to take some action, I started working on Plan B. I'm fortunate—my family is Indian, and I could easily step back into a culture where matchmaking is still widely practiced. I knew there were plenty of Indian parents who would love to introduce a cute lawyer to their son.

Why should I entrust my future to some random young man to find me and take an interest in me? So far that hadn't worked. Dating had lost its luster. I knew I didn't want to be single anymore. It was time to get proactive.

I decided to try a matchmaker. I'd heard about one in particular, and I liked the fact that he used a detailed questionnaire and interview to pair like-minded individuals. The questions fit with what I wanted to know about a potential husband, and I liked his being concerned with matching interests. Under the terms of his program, I knew that if after a few pairings nothing worked for me, he would remove me from the program. He believed that life was never meant to give unlimited options for unlimited amounts of time; instead he believed that people are under a biblical mandate to choose among available options in a timely fashion. Though I know this individual has had success in pairing others, our "matchmaker, matchmaker, make me a match" relationship did not work the magic I had hoped for. But I refused to give up or think that this episode was God's way of telling me to stop trying.

I hesitated to use e-Harmony.com or BigChurch.com, though I know they do have success matching couples. My concern with these sites is the lack of accountability. After talking to people and hearing their experiences, it seems like the Internet is often not being used by men to seriously search for a wife, but to test the limits of "wait and see if someone better comes along." I was afraid that many of the potential matches might be with men who weren't as serious as they thought. Even acknowledging that flaw, I still think sites like these are great avenues to pursue—it's much better than doing nothing and waiting for Mr. Right to fall from the sky!

I wanted to pursue the idea of agency and chose an Indian Christian Web agency because I knew that it would have a built-in accountability factor—parents. In many instances it is not the prospective bride or groom who has posted a listing, but parents looking on behalf of their son or daughter. Parents are a filter on the front end and only advance to their child the names of those they have pre-cleared as potential marriage material. This also allows the parents to do the rejecting without making the child look bad in the process.

Through this agency, I first met my future mother-in-law. She was searching for a wife for her son, who also had a legal background. Once again, the Indian culture more closely resembles how culture in America and Europe used to be: Mothers are actively involved in finding mates for their children. Even though the custom would have been for my parents to write to them, I wrote to her myself, and she and my future father-in-law were so impressed that they asked their son to correspond with me. And the rest is history.

Does this resemble an arranged marriage? Maybe, but it wasn't arranged in the way most people think of when they conjure up a picture of arranged marriage. We had the choice about whether we'd marry. And it's not like I showed up blindfolded on the back of a camel at the altar of First Presbyterian on my wedding day to meet my future husband for the first time. "Surprise!" I don't remember any exchange of goats or pigs for the dowry—in fact, there was no dowry at all.

Our arrangement was probably closer to being set up on a blind date, except the parents set up the blind date instead of a mutual friend. You meet the guy, but you're not obligated to see him after the first date. Just like a mutual friend who was there at the inception, parents are nosy and check on the progress from time to time.

From our first interactions through e-mail in July 2001, I asked him what he was looking for. What were his hopes for our relationship? Did he have any specific goals in mind in terms of how we interacted? Did he have a timetable in mind? Was he looking to marry this year, next year, sometime in the next decade? We talked and came up with a plan that would allow both of us to discover if we were compatible.

He flew to visit me in my hometown. I flew to visit him and his family. We went out on dates just like any other couple. We went to the Keys. We ate at restaurants. He kissed me, and I kissed him back. We flew back and forth to visit each other twice in August; he met my parents on Labor Day weekend; we visited a couple more times in September; and we were engaged in October with both of our families as witnesses.

And, yes, we fell in love—crazy in love. If we hadn't, we wouldn't have gotten married.

Agency can work to promote marriage. Others can be involved in your search for a spouse without it becoming a caricature of a forced arranged marriage. Perish the thought! If you're looking for a job, you enlist people in a position to help you. It's the same with looking for a spouse. It helps to have some friends in your corner instead of going it alone.

MAKE AGENCY WORK FOR YOU

You might not be from a different culture as I am and might not have the luxury of living in two worlds as I do. But agency can still work for you. The first thing I'd suggest is following a simple ethical framework on dating and/or courtship.

1. Don't date/court unless you are in a position to accept a proposal for marriage (i.e., anyone past high school).
2. Don't date/court with any motivation other than to discover within a short and reasonable length of time whether the other person is marriageable.
3. Don't date/court a man not in parity with yourself. (By parity, I mean someone who truly is your equal.) Get an agent/father figure who will act as a gatekeeper as well as scouting for mates.
4. Don't date/court anyone who is not in a position to extend an offer of marriage within a reasonable period of time (#1); and don't

date anyone who has different theories or motivations for dating, than the one suggested in #2.

This is not rocket science. This outline may seem rather perfunctory, and to some it may ring criminally unromantic. Most of us imagine that our paths with our future spouse will "intersect like the constellations, our eyes lock, and we will live forever after in the 'eternal springtime . . . [of] personal happiness.'"[10] We have visions of fun, relaxation, and laughter—long talks over coffee, walks on the beach at sunset, candlelit dinners. The romance of it all will point us toward destiny.

But following this framework doesn't negate the possibility of this kind of romance; my husband and I found lots of romance! Unfortunately, we as a culture have somehow come to believe that fun and responsible decision-making are polar opposites and that they can never occur together. We have come to believe that if anything is commenced with seriousness, formality, or expectations, it will lack spontaneity, and we will never find ourselves being romantically attached.

I'm not fighting against romance; I am fighting against what I call reckless romanticism, the kind of romanticism where we think we will be overjoyed with spontaneous surprises, one after the other. The danger of such recklessness is that little in the relationship matches any of our hopeful and grandiose expectations. Romance is vital for any lover's relationship, whether courtship or marriage. At its core, romance is not flowers or candy or a good candlelit meal; it is the feeling of being pursued by your lover. It's what we see in the Song of Songs.

Most women today are not pursued in a romantic sense because there is no infrastructure to praise or reward men for doing so. The number one complaint of women in college today is that men no longer ask them out for dates. They can't understand why they all just hang out in co-ed groups. This scenario has access breeding complacency written all over it.

Why should men pursue us if we make ourselves available for fellowship on all levels? The mystery of the female sex has completely disappeared; men have no need to pursue something they already know.

We will get more real romance if we abandon reckless romanticism with its unrealistic expectations of romance and destiny and instead use wisdom.[11] We will get more pursuit-style romance when we make the wise choice to limit access from the beginning. If we want men to pursue us, they must first feel alone and use that loneliness as an impetus to seek us out. When access to women is limited, men have the glory of having accomplished something by fighting for it or working for it. Their very nature and desire for conquest resists having someone who came too easily. I believe that when we as women participate in a no-commitment, casual, and lighthearted fashion from the inception of a relationship, we are actually insuring more heartache down the road.

Following this framework will not only tame men to behave like men, but it will help us save valuable time we cannot afford to lose. It will cull out the riffraff after the first date or two and will reduce the amount of heartache we suffer. Here are some thoughts to keep in mind if you pursue agency.

Use a strong agent.

Even though you may not live with your parents (which heartily I recommend as the better choice among the alternatives for single women), make a prospective husband establish an immediate relationship with your father or a father figure.

One obvious benefit to this is that if you have a hard time issuing ultimatums (it's time to commit or get lost), your father will not hesitate. It also establishes an order to your relationships. There are always rules to follow; it is only in the absence of rules that disorder occurs. Our God is the God of order. Make your dating/courting orderly by both initiating and relying on an agent other than yourself. Use the daddy God gave you!

Of course it doesn't always go as you plan. At one point a young man in another state had been calling me for a couple of months. He was obviously interested in me; we spent hours on the phone every Sunday afternoon. But I got tired of giving him free fellowship and killing his sense of aloneness, inhibiting his duty to pursue a wife. I decided to take action by having my father ask his intentions the next time he called.

I drafted a disarming script for my father. Dad practiced the script and was up for the task. If the young man said that he wanted to be friends with me, my father would ask him why there were no friends available in his hometown. If the young man said that he intended to pursue a romantic relationship, my father would ask him when the two of them should meet. And lastly, if the young man said he wasn't sure of his intentions, my father would inform him that he could call back and talk to him when he figured out what his intentions were. All possible outcomes to the conversation were accounted for.

I think my father may have been looking forward to this call just a little bit too much. Later on that week another male friend called from out of state, and my father applied the rehearsed lecture to him. While I was out that evening, my younger sister quickly realized the mix-up, made a mad dash for another phone, got my father to get off immediately, apologized to this other young man, and recommended that he disregard everything that he had just heard.

Had this worked as originally planned, I would have had resolution. I wouldn't be wasting my time if my friend wasn't serious about marriage. He might have realized the necessity of acting more quickly. Even if he had balked and refused to answer, he could call back when he was more prepared to give an answer. Whether I would still be available is another story. Having access denied, he would have no choice but to figure out what his intentions were and declare them. If he had no intentions toward marriage, then I had my answer. Either way I'd be better off knowing rather than guessing where the relationship was going.

Use your agent as a scout.

Have your agent actively look for a husband on your behalf. Ask him to keep an eye out for someone who might be suitable and to introduce you if someone comes to mind. It doesn't make sense to place this decision into the hands of someone who has no legal, moral, or ethical binding to you. Your father/father figure has your best interest in mind and at heart.

Barbara Dafoe Whitehead warns us, "The new single woman who is looking for a husband in the [new "relationship"] system can't allow men to set the pace and timing of her search. If she does, she is limiting her opportunity to reach her goal of marriage sooner rather than later."[12]

Want to get married sooner rather than later? You have to take some control in your search! Enlisting agency is only to your benefit.

Having an agent does not mean that your preferences or desires will no longer count. In the whole of Western history, the consent of the couple involved has been a necessary element in the validity of marriage. The caricature of forced arranged marriages is just that—an exaggeration. Even five thousand years ago, Rebekah's consent was required before she went to marry Isaac. In Reformation Europe, criminal sanctions and fines were often levied against parents who coerced children into unwanted engagements or withheld consent for monetary gain (dowry).[13] Having an agent on your side doesn't trump your preferences but actually gives you more bargaining power.

The reason I do not limit scouting or agency to biological fathers alone is because many of us do not come from Christian homes, or our fathers do not want to be involved. Find other trusted persons, such as wise and reliable married couples with good, well-disciplined children. At my former church, Bob and Libba Frey opened their home regularly to Christian women and were actively involved in praying for each woman to be married. Within a year after four of us young women became friends with this couple, three of us were married or engaged.

If you look to someone other than your own father, make sure they share your principles and convictions on the issue of protracted singleness. If your parents are not believers, I highly recommend the idea of surrogate spiritual fatherhood. Again, search carefully for someone to fulfill this role in your life. The surrogate you choose must understand the seriousness of what you're asking in order to be sympathetic to your plight of protracted singleness. Otherwise, be prepared for lectures on how you, too, can be a "gifted" single person.

Don't limit agency to fathers and father figures. Take advantage of matchmakers and Internet sites such as e-Harmony, Match.com, or BigChurch.com. Organizations such as It's Just Lunch, Great Expectations, or Good Genes, Inc. provide services to the marriage-minded. Many of these allow you to specify preferences and to search only for those who fit a certain profile, age bracket, professional or educational status, or denomination.

One more warning about accountability: Be cautious when there is no accountability for men to make wise decisions quickly. These sites do attract men who just love to ponder their options, much like standing in front of a vending machine. With so many options, some men cannot (or will not) make up their mind.

Agency will discourage disparity.

One of the benefits of calling as it was practiced in the early 1900s was that it usually ensured equality or parity. Because the woman's family issued the call, they decided who was worthy of their daughter. Under that system, it was the man who was in the somewhat vulnerable position of deciding whether the call was to visit someone in parity with him, someone with whom he could see a life together. If so, he could respond to the invitation; if not, he could decline and not know when the next call would come. (Sounds a lot like the waiting by the phone women do today, doesn't it?)

Dating has turned the tables. A man can pursue a woman well out of his league, and she often feels she has no choice but to say yes because by saying no she's stuck wasting more time waiting for the phone to ring again. Because access to women is so available and because there is no parental gatekeeper to impress, there is a perverse incentive for men to aim higher than what they're really worth. We often silently wonder, *How did he get her?* when we see an average, ho-hum kind of man with an outstanding woman. Rarely do we question how *she* got *him*. There just aren't that many cocktail waitresses married to brain surgeons.

Because we as women have to wait for the call to go out on a date, and because we have to wait for the man to propose marriage, we often spend years dating and being frustrated with less-than-worthy candidates. We—both men and women—are wasting each other's time in an endless cycle of systematic mismatches. Agency offers a solution.

An agent—especially a father or father figure—provides gatekeeping on the front end. The gatekeeper can tell a prospective suitor there is no parity—in background, educational status, ambitions, looks, societal standing, or money. He can tell the guy to take a hike, before you've wasted your time. I know this sounds discriminating and strikes at the very heart of our egalitarian, let's-not-judge, we're-all-equal philosophy—*but that philosophy ignores reality.* Many women who date in the current system feel like they are being gypped. And the reason they feel like they are being gypped is because they are. Women aren't dreaming about Mr. Right delivering pizzas at thirty-eight.

This kind of gatekeeping will influence men to aim wisely and timely for women on their level and who will appreciate them as they are, instead of wasting time and hoping to get lucky. It will save time for both men and women in the search for a marriage mate. It will reduce protracted singleness as the options are narrowed and a decision becomes a result of wise choice rather than unlimited possibilities.

Use your agent to establish a "scheduling order."

The main difference between dating and courtship is intention. Dating requires no intention to be stated, and the intentions behind dating are so varied, it's hard to know if you're on the same page. Courtship requires that purpose be stated up front.

As a lawyer, I often found the distinction much like the difference between state and federal courts. State court is unpredictable and scary, especially for conservative defense clients; federal court still has the rule of law and is more predictable. In state court, litigation (often frivolous) can drag on for years, until finally someone settles just to get the cobwebbed file out of the office; both parties go away with a bitter aftertaste. Perhaps the single most important factor between the two coexistent court systems is that in the federal court a judge is empowered and required *as soon as the litigation begins* to sit down with both of the parties to see if there is any possibility of a quick resolution, and if not, to institute a scheduling order, binding on all parties involved. The scheduling order sets time limits and specific dates for the end of discovery, motion deadlines, and the time of trial. The only way to get an extension is to establish "good cause" with the judge; occasionally both parties will pursue a joint motion for extension of time. The system is designed to keep both parties actively involved in working toward a successful completion of the litigation. All parties know where they stand and what is expected.

To me, the parallels are obvious. Following the dynamics of straightforward federal court litigation could be just what's needed to inject some clarity and responsibility into your dating relationships. Employ your father figure/gatekeeper to behave like the judge in federal court. As the final authority, the agent/father is empowered to tell a young man that he has to submit to his authority and display biblical masculinity before he can have continued access. If you feel uncomfortable laying down the scheduling order structure under which he must operate, this is the best place for a father figure to step in and set the rules. I know it sounds quaint and old-fashioned, but I would strongly suggest that it is always best to let the father/father figure have a talk with a young man who asks you out at the very beginning—and to continue a conversation throughout the course of the courtship.

While I am not suggesting that you make every date sign a contract in blood, I do suggest that you insist at the beginning of the relationship that the man take the initiative to establish the scheduling order if he wants to keep seeing you.

The end of the first date is ideal for this conversation. After the first date you will be in a better position to decide whether *you* want to explore where this relationship might lead. If you're not sure he'll call again, wait and bring it up if he calls for a second date. A second date usually implies that he wants to pursue some kind of relationship with you. Don't wait any longer. If you bring this up on the third date you now wear the lovely label of "pushing for a commitment."

By introducing this topic at the end of the first date or before beginning the second date, you can easily say that you are not pushing for a commitment. You may not want to be permanently committed to this man, but you are requesting the leadership you're entitled to, and you are handing him the reins to direct the course of this relationship. Feel free to tell him you're not trying to get him to say something he doesn't mean or commit to something he doesn't want to commit to, but you want his yes to be yes and his no to be no.

As the leader, he is responsible for establishing the purpose of your relationship and its goals (both short- and long-term). This way you are not put in the position of repeatedly asking him where you stand. As the leader, he can establish a time frame for evaluation and progress reports. Are you hitting it off? Are you attracted to each other? Can you see this relationship moving toward marriage? (Personally, I think two dates are more than enough to scratch someone off the list, and I would suggest three months is ample time to elicit a proposal. If it's not working out, you know, and it's time to move on.) By being up front and clear about your expectations and intentions, you both have the freedom to exit at any time—a relationship like this is not set in stone until wedding vows are spoken. With clear intentions it's much easier to guard both your heart and your purity.

With this self-imposed scheduling order, when time is up, it's up. Unless there's a "joint motion" for extension for good cause, it's time to move on. If it's been unsuccessful, heartbreak is kept to a minimum because you knew where you stood from the beginning. Neither one of you can say you wasted your time, since you agreed up front on the time line for the relationship. A scheduling order requires everyone involved to choose their words carefully—to say what they mean and speak the truth.

Help Your Parents Help You

My pastor used to joke that it takes two to make a marriage: a willing daughter and an anxious mother. Your parents are God's given agents for assistance in finding a husband.

Parents can pray for you.

One of the first things they can do for you is pray. Read what author Stormie Omartian writes in her book, *The Power of a Praying Parent*:

> When I think of the people I know who have experienced miserable marriages, abusive spouses, marital infidelity, multiple marriages, being married too late to have children, or who are unhappily single, one thing stands out in my mind: none of them had parents who interceded on their behalf for their mate and their marriage relationship.[14]

My mother-in-law prayed with and for my husband while we were courting, that God would reveal his intentions for us. Not everyone is fortunate enough to have believing parents. But even unbelieving parents generally have the best intentions at heart for their children. There is no reason not to engage parents to fulfill their biblical roles, whether they are believers or not.

Parents will sympathize and assist.

One simple way to assist parents in recapturing their responsibilities is to hand them a copy of this book. It will show them the dire circumstances under which women have to operate today and will not only garner sympathy but will encourage them to become actively involved in collaborating with you toward marriage. A dad's job shouldn't be just to write checks for the wedding, or a mom's to select the canapés. This book will help them see that their conduct during your adult years is vital to your entering marriage. They may even decide it is best for you to have a physical covering and let you move back in; they will certainly realize that they (or someone else) should act as your agent/gatekeeper/scout.

In *A Godly Form of Household Government*, Robert Cleaver outlined that family government has to have two ends in mind: Christian holiness and the "things of this life."[15] In order to bring children up in the nurture and admonition of the Lord, parents must "bring them up in some profitable & lawful calling, by which they may live honestly, & Christianly, & not be fruitless burdens of the earth . . . or commonwealth." They must also "provide for the disposing of them in marriage," "counseling them in their courtship and consenting to their marriage when they come of age and have chosen wisely among available spouses."[16] Parents should not give up on their duties of "counseling" their children toward marriage.

One couple met as undergraduates at Vanderbilt University and continued to date until she finished medical school. At that point the young man asked his father whether he thought he should marry this young woman. His father told him that he simply did not have a choice because this woman could never have those five years back again. It was too late to contemplate whether to marry because the question was already answered by his actions. The proper time to raise that question was at five weeks or months, not at five years. If only this were the kind of advice that all parents gave their children.

Agency works. It may sound old-fashioned at first; it may seem foreign. But agency establishes boundaries in our relationships with men, and boundaries provide safety. Just as small children play better and more happily in a well-defined space, within the boundaries of agency we can find comfort, freedom, and purpose to pursue the marriage God has called us to embrace.

CHAPTER 14

Inspiring Men to Biblical Manhood

*I*t is extraordinary that the first three recorded marriages in the Bible show the man's response to finding a wife. Adam was excited. Isaac found comfort. Jacob wept. You'd think that Eve, Rebekah, and Rachel would be the ones with their emotions spread across the pages of Scripture. I think two conclusions are appropriate.

First, when God established in Genesis 2:24 that "a man shall leave his father and his mother and hold fast to his wife," God firmly put the responsibility of marriage formation upon men. He can use the help of his parents and trusted agents, but it is ultimately his responsibility to make sure he marries. Since the leadership in this area falls squarely on men, it stands to reason that the man's feelings and emotions at the end of his efforts should be noted. Each one of these men had to do something, expend some effort, sacrifice something—whether it was Adam's rib donation, Isaac's expense of a caravan and costly gifts, or Jacob's long-distance journey and years of hard work. It is only appropriate that the man's duty in fulfilling his biblical obligations be remembered by noting his emotions at the successful completion of his duty.

Second, I think Moses wanted his audience to know that each one of these men acutely understood that it was "not good" to be alone. Their emotions confirm that we are designed for completion—for unity—with another human being, with a mate. The Bible gives us these glimpses into the everyday lives of the patriarchs to make clear that though God is the husband of his people, there is a deep ache within their souls designed to be fulfilled by a marriage partner, and a marriage partner *only*. This is why Moses mentioned that Isaac was forty years old when he got married, and that Rebekah comforted him. Isaac was uncomfortable being single that long and not having a wife. Admitting his longing did not undermine God's role in his life, nor did it show a supposed lack of contentment in God. It merely affirms our humanity and confirms that God made us "not . . . [to] be alone" (Genesis 2:18).

In the book of Judges, the story of Deborah shows that the proper response for women during a crisis of male leadership is to inspire men to better leadership. Despite his leadership position, Barak would go to war only if Deborah went with him. She responded by telling him the consequences of his decision to put her in front. The end of that story had already been written by God—Israel was assured victory. She asked him in essence, "Do you really want a woman to get the glory? It's your masculinity at stake here. Now, you choose."

God made men to be leaders—to pursue marriage and to seek a wife to ease their loneliness. The question is whether we, as women, will help men assume the leadership that God wanted them to have. How can we help them achieve their biblical potential? How will we help them fulfill their biblical duty to find a wife? Will we even try, or will we keep doing things just like before and then wonder why we are not married? We too have a choice to make.

INSPIRING MEN TO LEADERSHIP

Many men today are indulging in protracted adolescence. They play the dating game, buy more toys, and put marriage off for the future. And we let them. We live in a culture that tells us not to put off childish things but to embrace childhood for as long as possible. The excuse that "I'm not ready to get married" is no longer met with raised eyebrows but is accepted as a private choice of fully grown individuals to embrace life at their own pace, in their own time.

This has to stop. The prevailing attitude within the singles community to neglect marriage has huge consequences. If it continues to go unchecked, prolonged singleness will continue, and marriage and family will decline, both of which result in a weaker nation. When marriages aren't made and children aren't born, the birth rate drops, and portions of this nation's economy will fail.[1]

Ultimately there are no sound reasons or legitimate excuses why men—especially Christian men—are not getting married. Whatever the excuse *du jour*—lousy parents, divorced parents, protracted educational requirements, the high cost of living, fear of failure, misunderstanding the opposite sex—every excuse to put off marriage is a decision to stay single. Without accountability, nothing will change.

The Bible tells us that we will ultimately have to give an account for everything we did, including every careless word spoken, every malicious thought entertained (Matthew 12:36-37). Why we have believed that an indirect decision to remain single will be exempted from godly accountability is beyond reason and comprehension. Just as sexual sin affects other persons and includes them in sin, remaining single without the proper biblical predicate also affects another individual—the spouse you could have had. Remember what John Calvin said? The man who chooses to stay single (without a specific call from God) is guilty of "stealing" a husband from a wife.

Single men do not believe they will have to give an account for their delay, and they chafe at such a suggestion. But that's true of everyone. We all want to escape giving an account for our wrongdoing. It's uncomfortable! We've been conditioned to avoid such an accounting at all costs; everything in America is stacked toward shirking responsibility, and as Americans we readily buy the notion that it is always someone else's fault, never our own. It is easier to point the finger at someone else or to rationalize that God must have really wanted this delay of protracted singleness. We Christians are really not that different from the world; we too believe that none of our personal decisions regarding marriage should be challenged.

Unfortunately, we cannot expect anything better from a culture where the concept of marriage is a privatized one. In other words, marriage is treated as the private property of the two people involved, and who cares about everyone else? In that atmosphere, whether someone marries responsibly, delays marriage, or never marries, it is a privatized individual matter—free from accountability or challenge. People simply choose to believe that no one else has a stake in their choice. The problem in the Christian world is that now we have theology to reinforce that selfish school of thought.

The truth is that marriage is a social institution, not just a private relationship. The cost of a failed marriage (either through divorce or through its not having occurred at all) is a public cost. Singleness is not purely a private choice, but one that has a public cost because it fails to form a family. It costs someone a spouse, it costs us our own children, it costs grandparents grandchildren, and it fails to replenish the church nursery.

Erasmus said it well in his famous essay *In Praise of Marriage*: "[W]hat is more hateful than a man who, as though born for himself alone, lives for himself, looks out for himself, is sparing or lavish for himself, loves no one and is loved by no one? Indeed, should not such a monster be thought fit to be driven away from the general fellowship of mankind."[2] In other words, he saw those who willfully choose singleness as useless drones and fruitless burdens on this earth who have no sense of obligation to follow the familial patterns of their parents or to sacrifice for another.

Women, our biggest challenge in holding men accountable and inspiring them to biblical manhood is that they often don't know any better. They don't understand that this issue goes beyond personal choice to being held accountable by God for failing to pursue his will for their lives. We have no choice but to educate men. I think it would certainly be better if it came from ministers, church leaders, parents, or other male friends, but many of them are not particularly aware of the problem either.

Even if you are not educating your own Mr. Right, you may have brothers, family members, coworkers, and other male friends with whom you can speak frankly about these things. Remember that one of the things Deborah did to inspire Barak to take leadership was to warn him that his failure to lead would result in a woman getting the credit and glory that would otherwise be his. Deborah told him the consequences of his failure to lead. We must warn men of the accountability they will face and the consequences of their inaction. And think of your girlfriends: by inspiring men we know to exercise leadership, we are helping their future husbands.

So how do we do this in practical terms? As tempting as it may be to hit them over the head with this book, that probably won't work. Let's start by looking at some things we shouldn't do.

WHAT WE SHOULDN'T DO

We must not do nothing.

Something must change. The system we have isn't working. It can be scary to be on the front lines when making a change, but the results are worth it. Remember, the current school of thought tells us to do nothing and to expect God to pick up the pieces. Maintaining the status quo will only keep us in the status quo—being single (and we've already decided that's no fun).

There is no shortage of men; one woman's gain is not usually another woman's loss. This is not a zero-sum game or a race to the bottom. The only thing that there will be a shortage of are good Christian men if good Christian women aid and abet these men in prolonging their adolescence. If we want godly, Christian men, we must inspire them to be godly, Christian men. Doing nothing will leave us with exactly that—nothing.

We must not keep silent.

It's easy to think that if you demand biblical leadership from men, they'll run away screaming, and you'll never have a date again. But keeping silent and upholding the status quo is not the solution. In my late twenties, when I started employing some of these "hardball" tactics and being honest with men, their reaction wasn't to run. I can think of two men in particular who sincerely wanted to know what I thought good dating leadership looked like.

I dated one of them for two months, encouraging his leadership and knowing that at the three-month mark we were going to have a serious talk and would either end the relationship or buy a diamond ring. We used that time to cultivate a friendship, enjoy each other's company, and discover whether we would make a good match. It didn't work out because we had different views on money, ambition, and lifestyle. But there was no deception because our intentions were clear and honorable and both of us were working toward a resolution.

WHAT WE SHOULD DO

Limit the access men have to you.

I've said it before and I'll say it again, *limited access to women produces a desire from men to pursue marriage in a more timely and purposeful man-*

ner. When something (or someone) is readily available at little cost, there's little desire to pursue it and give it great value.

Employing an agent and enlisting the help of your father or a father figure is only to your benefit. As men are faced with an authority in this situation, they usually rise to the challenge. A man's being in an ongoing relationship with your father at the same time that he is dating you can inspire him to greatness. As one man said, "There are so few men out there for me to look up to. Everywhere I look I see men—even Christian men—failing miserably in their marriages and their careers. Knowing my wife's father has given me hope that it is possible to be a great Christian man who follows God and does the right thing. He's the kind of man I want to be."

Knowing that you're not readily available and waiting by the phone communicates to a man that you are valuable—he's going to have to prove himself to gain access to you. Men love to rise to a challenge!

The woman who refuses to participate in the current dating-poker game and holds herself to a higher standard not only saves herself wasted time, effort, energy, emotions, and often hurt feelings and disappointment, but she also will have an effect on the advancement of marriage. Motivating other women to accept the wisdom of dismissing leadership-deficient men will strengthen the overall cause of early marriages; even one woman has the power of change.

Every time a man is turned away for refusing to provide leadership, he is required to compete just a little bit harder for a slightly narrower pool of women. Competition alone will force compromise and concession according to the basic laws of supply and demand. The price for these other women just went up. The man then has no choice but to reexamine whether the price tag offered by the first woman who comes with a catch was really that unreasonable. Be strong! If you capitulate to the old patterns, you know very well you have no guarantee of marriage. You have nothing to lose by limiting a man's access to your life on the condition of demonstrated and verbalized leadership.

Ask for accountability.

Geographical mobility makes accountability difficult in today's world. We meet men from other places, and we don't know other people who can vouch for them. We don't have access to families or friends who know them best.

You can ask for accountability (and have your agent do the same). Asking questions is the best way to learn something. And asking specific questions is even better. Ask about dating history. Ask him why he's chosen to be single this long. Ask why he wants to date you—is he looking for something fun and casual, or is he looking for something permanent?

I would often tell men I dated that because they were over thirty and still unmarried, they lacked biblical leadership that requires securing a wife. They should have to explain why they are still single. Here's what's surprising: Asking these kinds of questions and demanding this kind of accountability doesn't make them run. Sure, some of them will. But when a man of thirty-five who hadn't dated for the past ten years asked my thirty-two-year-old friend for a date, she confronted him about it. "For every guy like you, there has been some woman dying on the vine like me. What excuse do you have for not pursuing a wife sooner?" This man did not run out of the restaurant but actually confessed that indeed he should have sought marriage!

Single at the age of thirty-four, my friend Anna desperately wanted to be married. Her boss asked if she'd be interested in dating "a very godly forty-five-year-old" lawyer. Her response? "If this man is so godly, why isn't he married by now?" She explained that she wasn't about to "reward a slothful forty-five-year-old man with someone eleven years his junior," but that she could recommend some woman who was well over forty, had lost the beauty of her youth, and would have trouble conceiving. She explained that this was the kind of candidate for this man since his inaction in finding a wife had caused this outcome for some other woman.

While her response may seem harsh, it's fair. There was a time, not too long ago, when women refused to go out with a man who had the reputation of being a cad. We need to start thinking in terms of godly accountability, not open-ended mercy.

Be careful about being "friends."

Can men and women be friends? In limited circumstances they can. But many suggest that this is a nearly impossible feat. They sometimes end up risking emotional purity. For all the talk about the feasibility of

endships, there seem to be a lot of "just friends" who keep
'hether men and women can be friends isn't the issue.

... the bigger question in this debate is, *should women befriend men?* It depends because I don't think it's always to our benefit to be friends. The fellowship and friendship men receive from women is very different from what they receive from men. In fact, I would suggest that perhaps the friendship men receive from women is partly responsible for upsetting their search for a wife. In other words, the friendship women give men can actually be a stumbling block to marriage.

If men don't ever feel loneliness for a wife because women provide them with the affirmation generally bestowed by a spouse, that does little to motivate them to take action toward marriage. While many people believe it's better to be friends first and see if anything more develops, I have to wonder if it more often results in marriages being prevented.

While these friendships can be pure, an abundance of male-female friendships can perhaps clog up the spouse-shaped void and destroy a powerful incentive to search for a spouse. We have to stop and ask if we are really being friends with men by being their friends. A friend generally cares about the other's long-term happiness and prosperity. A woman who sees her short-term friendship with a young man as an impediment to his willingness or urgency to search for long-term friendship in a wife may want to reconsider the terms of that friendship. Often it is the scarcity of female company that inspires men to act sooner rather than later. Men often do not want us because they get too much of us—they don't realize that anything is missing.

Rethink your single adult ministry.

We must consider the possibility of rethinking or even dropping single adult ministry (SAM) at church. I know this may sound radical, but many SAMs are built on the faulty foundation that marriage is optional, and their very existence serves to undermine our ability to marry. It is often just another avenue for us to sell our fellowship for free with little or nothing to show for it.

Most SAMs exist because churches believe that putting all the singles together in a vacuum is a way for singles to meet and that a number of marriages will happen as a result. But we must be honest about the fact that such ministries can be counterproductive for women in many instances.

Think about it this way. Men who are determined to find a wife will find one regardless of any program the church facilitates. Is it possible that the continued existence of this ministry only cripples the rest of the men who lack the same amount of initiative to find a wife? Remember, the pool of men in SAMs generally represents those men who after four (or more) years of college with constant access to marriageable women did not secure a wife. With that in mind, the existence of such a ministry may actually feed the cycle of protracted singleness. By virtue of its existence, these young men are lulled into a false security that there will always be a pool of good Christian women at any given time.

Moreover, with every vestige of aloneness removed, who needs a wife? Would someone really need a wife if he could survive on a steady succession of SAM bowling nights, game nights, movie nights, camping weekends, ice cream socials, ski trips, small groups, Bible studies, community groups, supper clubs, spring retreats, fall retreats . . . and never face a waking moment alone in his home?

Perhaps you are fortunate enough to be part of a SAM that preaches the whole will of God on marriage and singleness. If that is the case, and you are not only encouraged about the benefits of marriage but are taught that it is a duty to pursue marriage, you are fortunate. However, if you are in a ministry that looks at marriage as merely an option, preaches neutrality on the concept of marriage, glorifies singleness, or even discourages its members from moving toward marriage by plying them with a steady stream of activities, then you should prayerfully consider whether somewhere else in your church body is a better place for you in the long run.

Be the kind of woman who will be an asset to her future husband.
One of the first things taught in law school is that "one who wants equity must do equity." That's a biblical concept. We as women should try to remain as blameless and faultless as possible. I'm not talking about perfection but about maximizing your potential so that men perceive you as desirable. Do not let bad decisions on your part limit your opportunities for marriage.

If we want men to reach their full biblical potential, we should strive for the same. I think most men are searching for women who are smart, intelligent, good conversationalists, intriguing, educated, able to speak their minds, and yes, beautiful. Women should aspire to be these things so that men's desire to pursue is kindled.

While I do not buy the commonplace assumption that most men are looking for dummies who look good in a negligee, men do want attractive women. There is a reason that Scripture tells us that Jacob thought Rachel was "beautiful in form and appearance" (Genesis 29:17). There is a reason that Esther was primped. There is a reason that Naomi drew Ruth a perfumed bubble bath before she went to meet Boaz. Every woman is created in God's image. Develop your assets, and pay attention to how you look. The development of physical beauty is not in opposition to spiritual beauty. Both can be developed at the same time.

Some women are happy to play at the dating game, stringing men along and breaking their hearts. We must be honest and admit that men don't hold all the blame for the way things are. As Christian women, let's act in a manner according to our high calling and be godly women who behave well.

Educate others.

Think about the people you know—girlfriends, sisters, parents, brothers, cousins, friends, coworkers. How many people do you know who are affected by protracted singleness? I'm guessing that you know many who have felt its effect on one level or another.

We have a responsibility to tell others the truth. God has designed us for marriage, and he put the desire for it into our hearts. You are not wrong for being dissatisfied with your single state. You are not wrong to want more from the men you date. You are not wrong to pursue marriage.

Conclusion: Looking Ahead

The ideas presented in this book are so old they are new again. This book is only radical when compared with the prevailing wisdom of the last thirty years. It is commonplace when judged against the whole of history.

If you have read this far, I assume your reaction will either be "hate it" or "love it." No one walks away from my material lukewarm. Seek the Lord, and ask him to show you what is right as you continue to think and talk about your singleness. Scripture promises us that God gives wisdom generously to those who ask it, without finding fault (James 1:5).

I want women to be married. Marriage is wonderful. I love waking up every morning next to my husband—and sometimes waking up earlier than expected as little feet patter into our room. I love riding to church in the passenger seat and having a hand to hold during the service. I look forward to the passing of years and what they will bring, rather than anticipating each birthday with dread. I love having a date every weekend. I love the freedom to have legitimate sex whenever we want (and obviously we do considering my fertility rate during these first three years of marriage!). I have a husband with whom I can share my deepest thoughts and affections. We are building a life together and are creating a legacy to leave for our children.

I cannot apologize for wanting this same wonderful life for my daughters and for each single woman who reads this book.

May God guide you and bless you as you ponder the duty to marry and pursue the highest calling given to men and women.

Discussion Guide

CHAPTER 1:
WHAT THE BIBLE SAYS ABOUT MARRIAGE

1. Grab a Bible and read Genesis 1—3. If you've been a Christian for very long, you're probably familiar with the story of Creation. It's easy to skim something when we know it well. Take your time, and read it slowly. What stands out to you about Adam, Eve, and their relationship? What is God's revealed will (his intended purpose) for them?

2. How have you experienced loneliness as a single woman?

3. Since you picked up this book, it's a safe assumption that you're dissatisfied with singleness and would rather be married. Martin Luther said, "God knows what is better for you than you yourself. . . . If you deem it otherwise . . . you neither understand nor believe God's word and work." Do you believe that God knows what's best for you in regard to marriage? What's keeping you from believing that God has said he wants you to be married?

4. "God designed us to feel incomplete without a spouse." Is this a new idea for you? Explain your reaction to this statement.

5. In what ways have you struggled with your motivation for working? Have you ever wondered, "Who is it all for?"

6. What are your dreams for having a family?

CHAPTER 2:
WHAT THE BIBLE SAYS ABOUT BEING SINGLE

1. What are the exceptions to singleness that Jesus listed in Matthew 19?

2. Do you fit any of those exemptions? Explain your answer.

3. Think about being called by God for service. All believers are called to serve God—you're no exception. Does the service you're called to preclude marriage? If so, how?

4. What are the reasons Paul gives for delaying marriage or remaining single? How does knowing the context for 1 Corinthians 7 and viewing Scripture as a whole change how you read this passage?

5. Do you have any additional questions about what the Bible says about singleness? Pray that God will give you answers and will lead you to godly teachers for guidance.

CHAPTER 3:
HISTORICAL VIEWS ON MARRIAGE AND SINGLENESS

1. Have you ever felt like it's your fault that you're single?

2. Think about the changes in society and culture in regard to marriage. What has surprised you the most? Do you see any other changes not mentioned in this chapter?

3. Do you think that marriage is a duty? How so?

4. Make a list of pros and cons for marrying in your youth, and do the same for marrying later in life. What do you discover from comparing your lists?

5. Come up with a succinct statement that describes the paradigm shift that has occurred in thinking about marriage.

CHAPTER 4:
THE LACK OF MALE LEADERSHIP: THE TRUE CAUSE OF PROTRACTED SINGLENESS

1. How have you most often seen men portrayed in the media?

2. Do you agree that as a culture we have failed to produce a large number of marriage-material men? Why or why not?

3. In what ways have you been required to be independent?

4. Are you looking for male leadership in your life? Explain your answer.

5. How did your parents prepare you for marriage? Was it something they did by the example of being married themselves, or did they intentionally prepare you to be married?

CHAPTER 5:
WHAT WE'VE BEEN TAUGHT

1. What advice have you received about being single?

2. What have you been taught to do with your desire to be married?

3. Look at each of the four messages presented in this chapter. When have you encountered these messages? How have you responded?

CHAPTER 6:
THE "GIFT" OF SINGLENESS AND THE
SOVEREIGNTY OF GOD

1. How have you thought about marriage in the past? Is it something you've thought just "happens," or have you viewed marriage as something to pursue?

2. It's vital that we define *God's sovereignty* and *God's will*. Take a minute to define each of those terms. Are you clear on what they mean, or do you still have questions?

3. In your own words, explain the singleness position endorsed by much of the contemporary church.

4. Do you have any additional questions as a result of this common position other than the ones posed in the chapter?

5. Define outcome-based theology. What are the dangers of endorsing such theology?

6. What choices have resulted in your singleness?

CHAPTER 7:
"WAIT ON THE LORD"

1. Where are you when it comes to waiting? Are you at the beginning of a wait where it doesn't seem too bad, or have you been waiting for a while?

2. What costs have you had to pay as a result of waiting for marriage?

3. "Marriage is the norm God established from the beginning. Marriage is what we're to pursue unless God specifically calls us to remain single." Have you faced teaching that says otherwise? Have you fallen prey to the backwards thinking of staying single unless God orders marriage?

4. Are you beginning to see that marriage is something God wants for you? How is your thinking beginning to change?

CHAPTER 8:
"JESUS IS ALL YOU NEED"

1. Are you comfortable saying no when someone asks if you're seeing anyone special, or do you usually add an explanation?

2. It's time to be honest. How do you feel about being single—still? Are there some safe people with whom you can begin to be honest about the pain of protracted singleness?

3. How can you be a safe person for other women dealing with this issue? How can you encourage others to express their true feelings?

4. Do you identify yourself in the quote by Dr. Kass? If so, how?

5. Think about the spouse-shaped hole God designed in you. What have you been told to fill it with? What have you tried to plug it with? Is that working?

6. How have you experienced discontentment with singleness? After reading this chapter, do you see those feelings in a new light?

CHAPTER 9:
"BEING SINGLE = KNOWING AND
SERVING GOD BETTER"

1. Have you ever wondered, *What in the world do I have to do to get married?* What kinds of answers have you received?

2. How is your time spent as a single person? Do you think you have lots of leftover time for God without a husband or children?

3. Think about the kinds of ministry you're involved in. How would being married and having a family affect your ministry?

4. Do you think you know God better because you're single? Explain your answer.

5. God has revealed himself through family relationships. In what ways has God revealed himself to you?

CHAPTER 10:
"SINGLE = CELIBATE"

1. How have you dealt with your desire for sex?

2. Define celibacy.

3. Do you think you have the gift of celibacy? Why or why not? And if you do believe you have the gift of celibacy, how have you been serving God such that marriage and family seem impractical?

4. How does preaching abstinence without the promise of marriage remove hope?

5. Do you think the desire for sex is reason enough to marry? Explain your answer.

6. Luther said, "Whoever finds himself [or herself] unsuited to the celibate life should . . . strike out in God's name and get married." How unsuited do you feel to the celibate life? How do you know from day to day that you are unsuited to it?

Chapter 11:
A Few More "Easy" Answers

1. Which of these answers have you faced in the past?

2. Does having a response ready make you feel prepared to face them again in the future?

3. It seems like there's always one person in particular who offers the same easy answer over and over. It might help to draft a script of what you can say the next time you find yourself face to face with that person.

4. So many of these answers stem back to the "biggies" covered in Chapters 6-10. As you're faced with new answers, see if you can trace them back to one of these big ideas. It will help you know how to respond.

Chapter 12:
Saying No to the Dating Game

1. What's your dating history? When did you start dating? What were you told about it?

2. In what ways have you rationalized dating's lack of efficiency?

3. Have you experienced inequality in dating? When? What happened?

4. In what ways have you had to guard your heart as you've dated?

5. If you're in a dating relationship, what questions do you need to ask? Do time limits need to be set?

6. Do you need to say no to a relationship right now? Ask your friends—sometimes they can see the need for this more clearly than you can on your own.

Chapter 13:
Enlisting Agency

1. "Access breeds complacency." Do you agree? Spend some time thinking about this idea and how you've seen this played out.

2. Is agency appealing to you? Explain your answer.

3. Reread the ethical framework for dating/courtship. Is this something you think you could adhere to? Why or why not?

4. It might help to decide with several girlfriends that you are going to stick to this framework together. How could you hold each other accountable?

5. If you decide to pursue agency, come up with a specific plan for each part of the process: Choose a strong agent. Use your agent as a scout. Watch out for disparity. Establish a scheduling order.

6. What do you need to do to help your parents help you?

CHAPTER 14:
INSPIRING MEN TO BIBLICAL MANHOOD

1. Read the story of Deborah and Barak in your Bible (Judges 4—5). What stands out to you from their story?

2. How can you begin to educate the men in your life? Make a list of the men you regularly spend time with. What does each of these men need to know specifically about the kind of leadership women want and need from them?

3. How can you limit the access that men have to you, especially men who might be "marriage material"?

4. Are you friends with many men? In what ways do you think your friendship helps them? Can you see any ways in which it might be a hindrance to their desire to get married? This is hard to think about, but take some time and pray about those friendships and whether to continue them.

5. If you're involved in a single adult ministry, it's time for an evaluation. What does that ministry teach about singleness and marriage? Is it in line with the whole of Scripture? It might be a good idea to sit down with someone in leadership and get a clear picture of your ministry's goals and direction.

6. Do you need to make some changes in order to be the kind of woman men want to pursue? Are you presenting yourself in the best possible way—from your speech, your tone of voice, and your attitude to your clothes, your haircut, and your posture? Do you need to work through any issues or gain some maturity before you're ready to be married?

CONCLUSION:
LOOKING AHEAD

1. What have you learned from reading this book? What two or three things have changed the most in your view of singleness and marriage?

2. Each woman has the power to affect change. What's your next step as you move toward marriage? If you've read this book with a friend or two, how can you continue to hold each other accountable in the future?

Notes

INTRODUCTION

1. Jason Fields and Lynne M. Casper, *American's Families and Living Arrangements*, June 2001, Current Population Reports, P20-537, U.S. Census Bureau, pp. 9-11.

2. Dr. Sanjay Gupta, "Say 'I Do' to Health," *Time*, June 7, 2004, p. 134.

3. Linda J. Waite and Maggie Gallagher, *The Case for Marriage: Why Married People Are Happier, Healthier, and Better Off Financially* (New York: Doubleday, 2000), pp. 105-106.

4. David Popenoe and Barbara Dafoe Whitehead, *Age at First Marriage: What's Best?* in *The State of Our Unions, Part 2: Social Indicators of Marital Health & Wellbeing*, 2001; http://marriage.rutgers.edu/Publications/SOOU/TEXTSOOU 2003.htm#AgeatFirstMarriage.

CHAPTER 1

1. Dr. Albert Mohler, "Looking Back at 'The Mystery of Marriage'—Part I," August 19, 2004, http://www.crosswalk.com/news/weblogs/mohler/?adate=8/19/2004.

2. John Piper and Wayne Grudem, *Recovering Biblical Manhood and Womanhood* (Wheaton, Ill.: Crossway Books, 1991), p. 99.

3. John Calvin, *Commentaries on the Book of Genesis*, Vol. 1/1. Translated from the original Latin, and compared with the French edition, by Reverend John King (Grand Rapids, Mich.: Baker Book House, 1979), p. 97.

4. John Calvin, *Commentary on the Epistle of Paul the Apostle to the Corinthians*. Vol. 20/22. Translated from the original Latin, collated with the French edition, by Reverend John Pringle (Grand Rapids, Mich.: Baker Book House, 1979), p. 224.

5. Calvin, *Commentaries on the Book of Genesis*, p. 129.

6. Martin Luther, "The Estate of Marriage," in *Luther's Works*, Vol. 45, as found in Vol. 2 of *Christian in Society*, ed. W. I. Brandt (Philadelphia: Fortress Press, 1962), p. 37.

7. Calvin, *Commentaries on the Book of Genesis*, p. 129.

8. Ephesians 4:28 supports this idea—work is ordained not just for work's sake, but so we will be "doing honest work with [our] own hands, *so that [we] may have something to share with anyone in need*" (emphasis mine).

9. Lev Grossman, "Grow Up? Not so Fast," *Time* magazine, January 24, 2005, pp. 42-54.

10. Linda J. Waite and Maggie Gallagher, *The Case for Marriage: Why Married People Are Happier, Healthier, and Better Off Financially* (New York: Doubleday, 2000), pp. 105-106, 110-236.

11. Douglas Wilson, *Standing on the Promises* (Moscow, Ida.: Canon Press, 1991), p. 23.

12. Michael P. Orsi, "A Case for Earlier Marriage," *Homiletic & Pastoral Review*, October 2001.

13. Leland Ryken, *Worldly Saints: The Puritans as They Really Were* (Grand Rapids, Mich.: Zondervan, 1986), p. 48.

14. Calvin, *Commentary on the Epistle of Paul the Apostle to the Corinthians*, pp. 359-360.

CHAPTER 2

1. Craig L. Blomberg, *The New American Commentary: Matthew*, ed. David S. Dockery, Vol. 22 (Nashville: Broadman Press, 1992), p. 290.

2. Ibid.

3. Desiderius Erasmus, "In Praise of Marriage," as found in *Wing to Wing, Oar to Oar*, ed. Leon and Amy Kass (Notre Dame, Ind.: Notre Dame Press, 2000), p. 94.

4. Martin Luther, "The Estate of Marriage," in *Luther's Works*, Vol. 45, as found in Vol. 2 of *Christian in Society*, ed. W. I. Brandt (Philadelphia: Fortress Press, 1962), pp. 18-19.

5. Conversation with Pastor Duncan Rankin of Covenant Presbyterian Church in Oak Ridge, Tenn., who cited John Calvin.

6. Luther, "The Estate of Marriage," p. 21.

7. Ibid.

8. Simon J. Kistemaker, *New Testament Commentary: 1 Corinthians* (Grand Rapids, Mich.: Baker Books, 1993), p. 33.

9. Ibid., p. 239.

10. Ibid., pp. 239-240.

11. Ibid., p. 256.

12. John Calvin, *Commentary on the Epistle of Paul the Apostle to the Corinthians*. Vol. 20/22. Translated from the original Latin, collated with the French edition, by Reverend John Pringle (Grand Rapids, Mich.: Baker Book House, 1979), p. 223.

13. Ibid., pp. 252-253.

14. Kistemaker, *New Testament Commentary: 1 Corinthians*, p. 210.

15. Ibid., p. 219.

16. Gordon D. Fee, *The New International Commentary on the New Testament: The First Epistle to the Corinthians* (Grand Rapids, Mich.: Wm. B. Eerdmans, 1987), p. 284.

17. Ibid.

18. Ibid., p. 285.

19. Calvin, *Commentary on the Epistle of Paul the Apostle to the Corinthians*, p. 252.

20. Ibid.

21. Ibid.

22. Ibid., pp. 252-253.

23. Fee, *The New International Commentary on the New Testament: The First Epistle to the Corinthians*, p. 270.

24. Kistemaker, *New Testament Commentary: 1 Corinthians*, p. 240.

25. Fee, *The New International Commentary on the New Testament: The First Epistle to the Corinthians*, p. 334.

26. John Calvin, *Commentaries on the Book of Genesis*, Vol. 1/1. Translated from the original Latin, and compared with the French edition, by Reverend John King (Grand Rapids, Mich.: Baker Book House, 1979), p. 134.

27. Ibid., pp. 128-129.

CHAPTER 3

1. John Witte, Jr., *From Sacrament to Contract: Marriage, Religion, and Law in the Western Tradition* (Louisville: Westminster John Knox Press, 1997), p. 49.

2. Ibid.

3. Ibid.

4. Martin Luther, "The Estate of Marriage," in *Luther's Works*, Vol. 45, as found in Vol. 2 of *Christian in Society*, ed. W. I. Brandt (Philadelphia: Fortress Press, 1962), p. 18.

5. Witte, *From Sacrament to Contract: Marriage, Religion, and Law in the Western Tradition*, p. 111, citing *Institutes* (1559).

6. Calvin, *Commentary on the Epistle of Paul the Apostle to the Corinthians*, see generally; and Calvin, *Commentary on a Harmony of the Evangelists*, Vol. 16/22. Translated from the original Latin, and collated with the French edition, by Reverend John Pringle (Grand Rapids, Mich.: Baker Book House, 1979), see generally.

7. Dr. Albert Mohler, "Looking Back at 'The Mystery of Marriage'—Part 1," August 19, 2004, http://www.crosswalk.com/news/weblogs/mohler/?adate=8/19/2004.

8. See Doug Jones and Doug Wilson, *Angels in the Architecture* (Moscow, Ida.: Canon Press, 1998), p. 21.

9. Stephen G. Post, *More Lasting Unions: Christianity, the Family, and Society* (Grand Rapids, Mich.: Wm. B. Eerdmans, 2000), p. 83; see also Leland Ryken, *Worldly Saints: The Puritans as They Really Were* (Grand Rapids, Mich.: Zondervan, 1986), p. 44.

10. Ryken, *Worldly Saints: The Puritans as They Really Were*, p. 45.

11. Witte, *From Sacrament to Contract: Marriage, Religion, and Law in the Western Tradition*, pp. 83-86.

12. Westminster Larger Catechism, Questions 98-196. http://www.freepres.org/WCFLarge2.htm (accessed February 22, 2001).

13. Hans J. Hillerbrand, *The Oxford Encyclopedia of the Reformation*, Vol. 3 (New York: Oxford University Press, 1996), p. 20.

14. Ryken, *Worldly Saints: The Puritans as They Really Were*, citing John Cotton.

15. Witte, *From Sacrament to Contract: Marriage, Religion, and Law in the Western Tradition*, citing *The Early Works of Thomas Becon*, S.T.P., Vol. 2., ed. J. Ayre for the Parker Society, 3 vols. (Cambridge: University Press, 1993), pp. 532-533.

16. Witte, *From Sacrament to Contract: Marriage, Religion, and Law in the Western Tradition*, p. 144.

17. Ryken, *Worldly Saints: The Puritans as They Really Were*, p. 44.

18. William Gouge, *Of Domesticall Duties* (London 1622) (Norwood, N.J., Amsterdam: Walter J. Johnson, Theatrum Orbis Terrarum, Ltd., 1976), pp. 210-211.

19. Post, *More Lasting Unions: Christianity, the Family, and Society*, p. 83, citing Jeremy Taylor, "The Marriage Ring," in *Jeremy Taylor: Selected Works*, ed. T. K. Carroll (Mahway, N.J.: Paulist Press, 1990), pp. 261-267.

20. Ryken, *Worldly Saints: The Puritans as They Really Were*, p. 42.

21. Edmund Morgan, *The Puritan Family: Religion and Domestic Relations in Seventeenth-Century New England* (New York: Harper Torchbooks, 1944), p. 27.

22. Ibid., p. 145.

23. "The Family Timeline," *World Magazine*, May 20, 2000, p. 12.

24. Morgan, *The Puritan Family: Religion and Domestic Relations in Seventeenth-Century New England*, pp. 145-146.

25. Kay Hymowitz, *Ready or Not: What Happens When We Treat Children as Small Adults* (San Francisco: Encounter Books, 2000), p. 202.

26. Ibid.

27. Post, *More Lasting Unions: Christianity, the Family, and Society*, p. 79; and Morgan, *The Puritan Family: Religion and Domestic Relations in Seventeenth-Century New England*, p. 87.

28. Morgan, *The Puritan Family: Religion and Domestic Relations in Seventeenth-Century New England*.

29. Hans J. Hillerbrand, *The Oxford Encyclopedia of the Reformation*, Vol. 3 (New York: Oxford University Press, 1996), see generally.

30. Stephen Ozmint, *When Fathers Ruled: Family Life in Reformation Europe* (Cambridge, Mass.: Harvard University Press, 1983), see generally.

31. Witte, *From Sacrament to Contract: Marriage, Religion, and Law in the Western Tradition*, p. 149.

32. Ibid., see generally.

33. Ibid.

34. Post, *More Lasting Unions: Christianity, the Family, and Society*, p. 83, citing Jeremy Taylor, "The Marriage Ring," in *Jeremy Taylor: Selected Works*, ed. T. K. Carroll (Mahway, N.J.: Paulist Press, 1990), pp. 263, 265.

35. Witte, *From Sacrament to Contract*, see generally.

36. Ibid.

37. Ibid.
38. Ibid., p. 10.
39. Ibid., p. 199.
40. Ibid.
41. Ibid., p. 10.
42. Barbara Dafoe Whitehead, *Why There Are No Good Men Left: The Romantic Plight of the New Single Woman* (New York: Broadway Books, 2003), p. 25.
43. From "Marriage," www.encarta.msn.com/encyclopedia_761574825_3/Marriage.html.
44. Post, *More Lasting Unions: Christianity, the Family, and Society*, pp. 94-96.
45. Ibid.
46. Ibid.
47. Bradford Wilcox, "What's Next for the Marriage Movement?" *American Experiment Quarterly*, Summer 2002, p. 50.
48. Ibid.

CHAPTER 4

1. C. S. Lewis, "We Have No Right to Happiness," in *God in the Dock*, Part III, Chapter 9 (Grand Rapids, Mich.: Wm. B. Eerdmans, 1972).
2. Barbara Dafoe Whitehead and David Popenoe, *The State of Our Unions, Social Health of Marriage in America* (2002), National Marriage Project, p. 5.
3. Ibid., p. 3.
4. Doug Wilson, *Standing on the Promises*, (Moscow, Ida.: Canon Press, 1991), p. 15.
5. Allan Bloom, "Relationships," as found in ed. Leon and Amy Kass, *Wing to Wing, Oar to Oar* (Notre Dame, Ind.: Notre Dame Press, 2000), p. 45.
6. Wilson, *Standing on the Promises*, p. 166.
7. Bloom, "Relationships," p. 46.
8. Ibid., p. 47.
9. Carolyn Graglia, *Domestic Tranquility* (Dallas: Spence Publishing, 1998), p. 89.
10. Kay Hymowitz, *Ready or Not: What Happens When We Treat Children as Small Adults* (San Francisco: Encounter Books, 2000), p. 201.
11. Ibid., p. 207.
12. Ibid., p. 203.
13. Wilson, *Standing on the Promises*, p. 82.
14. Ibid., p. 94.
15. Ibid., pp. 9-10.
16. Ibid., p. 163.
17. Michael P. Orsi, "An Uncommon Policy Regarding Marriage," *Homiletic & Pastoral Review,* May 1999, pp. 56-61.
18. John MacArthur, "Reasons for Remaining Single, Part 1: Because of the World," radio program *Grace to You*, aired February 2003.

CHAPTER 5

1. Julia Duin, "Why Singles Boycott Churches," *Breakpoint Online*, Prison Fellowship Ministries, January 7, 2003.

2. Ellen Johnson Varughese, *The Freedom to Marry* (self-published by Joy Press, 1992), p. 34.

3. Kimberly Hartke, from an interview conducted July 24, 2001.

4. Focus on the Family, Colorado Statement on Biblical Sexual Morality.

CHAPTER 6

1. Al Hsu, *Singles at the Crossroads* (Downers Grove, Ill.: InterVarsity Press, 1997), p. 14.

2. Julia Duin, "No One Wants to Talk About It," *Breakpoint Online*, Prison Fellowship Ministries, January 20, 2003.

3. See Proverbs 5:18, Malachi 2:14-15, and Joel 1:8.

4. Justice Policy Institute Report, August 28, 2003; www.justicepolicy.org/article.php?id=242.

5. Hosea 9:10-17.

CHAPTER 7

1. Barbara Dafoe Whitehead, "The Plight of the High Status Woman," *Atlantic Monthly*, December 1999.

2. Linda J. Waite and Maggie Gallagher, *The Case for Marriage: Why Married People Are Happier, Healthier, and Better Off Financially* (New York: Doubleday, 2000), p. 29.

3. Lee Dye, "Why Are More Men Waiting to Marry?" quoting David Popenoe, http://abcnews.go.com/Technology/story?id=97920&page=1.

4. Gene Edward Veith, "Population Implosion," *World Magazine*, February 15, 2003, p. 13.

5. David Popenoe and Barbara Dafoe Whitehead, *State of our Unions 2000*, National Marriage Project, p. 14.

6. Veith, "Population Implosion," p. 13.

7. Ibid.

8. Ibid.

CHAPTER 8

1. Ruth Haley Barton, *Invitation to Solitude and Silence* (Downers Grove, Ill.: InterVarsity Press), p. 50.

2. Ibid., pp. 51-52.

3. Leon Kass, "Courtship," as found in ed. Don Eberly, *Building a Healthy Culture* (Grand Rapids, Mich.: Wm. B. Eerdmans, 2001), pp. 369-370.

4. Phone interview with Kimberly Hartke, True Love Ministries, July 24, 2001.

5. Barbara Dafoe Whitehead, *Why There Are No Good Men Left: The Romantic Plight of the New Single Woman* (New York: Broadway Books, 2003), p. 31.

6. Michael P. Orsi, "A Case for Earlier Marriage," *Homiletic and Pastoral Review*, October 2001.

7. Timothy Keller, sermon entitled "Gospel Community: Singleness, Marriage and Family: Part 1," Redeemer Presbyterian Church, New York City, November 2001.

8. Ibid.

9. Ellen Johnson Varughese, *The Freedom to Marry* (self-published by Joy Press, 1992), p. 46.

10. Keller, "Gospel Community: Singleness, Marriage and Family: Part 1."

CHAPTER 9

1. Douglas Wilson, *Standing on the Promises*, (Moscow, Ida.: Canon Press, 1991), p. 67.

CHAPTER 10

1. In a John Piper sermon entitled "Sexual Relations in Marriage," Bethlehem Baptist Church, Minneapolis, February 15, 1981.

2. Lauren Winner, "Sex and the Single Evangelical: The Church Lady vs. the 'Evangelical Whore.'" First published in 2000 and available at http://www.beliefnet.com/story/5/story_597_1.html (accessed June 30, 2005).

3. Julia Duin, "No One Wants to Talk About It," *Breakpoint Online*, Prison Fellowship Ministries, January 20, 2003.

4. Ibid.

5. Ibid.

6. My husband read this comment in an interview of Bobby Bowden in *GQ* magazine

7. Hans J. Hillerbrand, *The Oxford Encyclopedia of the Reformation*, Vol. 3 (New York: Oxford University Press, 1996), p. 21.

8. John Witte, Jr., *From Sacrament to Contract: Marriage, Religion, and Law in the Western Tradition* (Louisville: Westminster John Knox Press, 1997), p. 50.

9. Ben Witherington, III, *Conflict and Community in Corinth: A Socio-Rhetorical Commentary on First and Second Corinthians* (Grand Rapids, Mich.: Wm. B. Eerdmans, 1995), p. 180, note 4.

10. Steve Tracy (interview), "Sex and the Christian Single," *Christianity Today*, July 10, 2000.

11. John Calvin, *Commentaries on the Book of Genesis*, Vol. 1/1. Translated from the original Latin, and compared with the French Edition, by Reverend John King (Grand Rapids, Mich.: Baker Book House, 1979), p. 136.

12. Desiderius Erasmus, "In Praise of Marriage," as found in *Wing to Wing, Oar to Oar*, ed. Leon and Amy Kass (Notre Dame, Ind.: Notre Dame Press, 2000), p. 101.

13. Ibid.

14. Martin Luther, "The Estate of Marriage," in *Luther's Works*, Vol. 45, as found in Vol. 2 of *Christian in Society*, ed. W. I. Brandt (Philadelphia: Fortress Press, 1962), pp. 18-19.

15. Ibid., p. 18.

16. Ibid., pp. 44-48.

CHAPTER 12

1. David Popenoe and Barbara Dafoe Whitehead, *Age at First Marriage: What's Best?* in *The State of Our Unions, Part 2: Social Indicators of Marital Health & Wellbeing*, 2001; http://marriage.rutgers.edu/Publications/SOOU/TEXTSOOU 2003.htm#AgeatFirstMarriage.

2. Wendy Shalit, *A Return to Modesty* (New York: Touchstone, 1999), pp. 11, 91, 167.

3. Barbara Dafoe Whitehead, *Why There Are No Good Men Left: The Romantic Plight of the New Single Woman* (New York: Broadway Books, 2003), p. 45.

4. Henry Cloud and John Townsend, *Boundaries in Dating* (Grand Rapids, Mich.: Zondervan, 2000), p. 26.

5. Shalit, *A Return to Modesty*, pp. 11, 91, 167.

6. Whitehead, *Why There Are No Good Men Left*, p. 45.

7. Danielle Crittenden, *What Our Mothers Didn't Tell Us* (New York: Touchstone, 1999), p. 67.

CHAPTER 13

1. Beth Bailey, "From the Front Porch to the Back Seat," in *Wing to Wing, Oar to Oar*, ed. Leon and Amy Kass (Notre Dame, Ind.: Notre Dame Press, 2000), p. 31.

2. Danielle Crittenden, *What Our Mothers Didn't Tell Us* (New York: Touchstone, 1999), p. 54.

3. Bailey, "From the Front Porch to the Back Seat," p. 32.

4. Ibid., p. 35.

5. Barbara Dafoe Whitehead, *Why There Are No Good Men Left: The Romantic Plight of the New Single Woman* (New York: Broadway Books, 2003), p. 97.

6. Ibid., p. 14.

7. Ibid., pp. 30, 102.

8. Wendy Shalit, *A Return to Modesty* (New York: Touchstone, 1999), pp. 11, 91, 167.

9. John Calvin, *Commentary on the Epistle of Paul the Apostle to the Corinthians*. Vol. 20/22. Translated from the original Latin, collated with the French edition, by Reverend John Pringle (Grand Rapids, Mich.: Baker Book House, 1979), pp. 266-267.

10. Gary Thomas, "Romantic Follies," *Christian Single Magazine*, April 2000, citing Katherine Ann Porter.

11. Ibid.
12. Whitehead, *Why There Are No Good Men Left*, p. 169.
13. John Witte, Jr., *From Sacrament to Contract: Marriage, Religion, and Law in the Western Tradition* (Louisville: Westminster John Knox Press, 1997), p. 84.
14. Stormie Omartian, *The Power of a Praying Parent* (Eugene, Ore: Harvest House, 1995), pp. 167-168.
15. Witte, *From Sacrament to Contract: Marriage, Religion, and Law in the Western Tradition*, p. 168.
16. Ibid., p. 169.

CHAPTER 14

1. Michael P. Orsi, citing B. Wattenberg, "Hiding the Population Implosion," *New York Post*, March 7, 2001, p. 27.
2. Desiderius Erasmus, "In Praise of Marriage," in *Wing to Wing, Oar to Oar*, ed. Leon and Amy Kass (Notre Dame, Ind.: Notre Dame Press, 2000), p. 101.